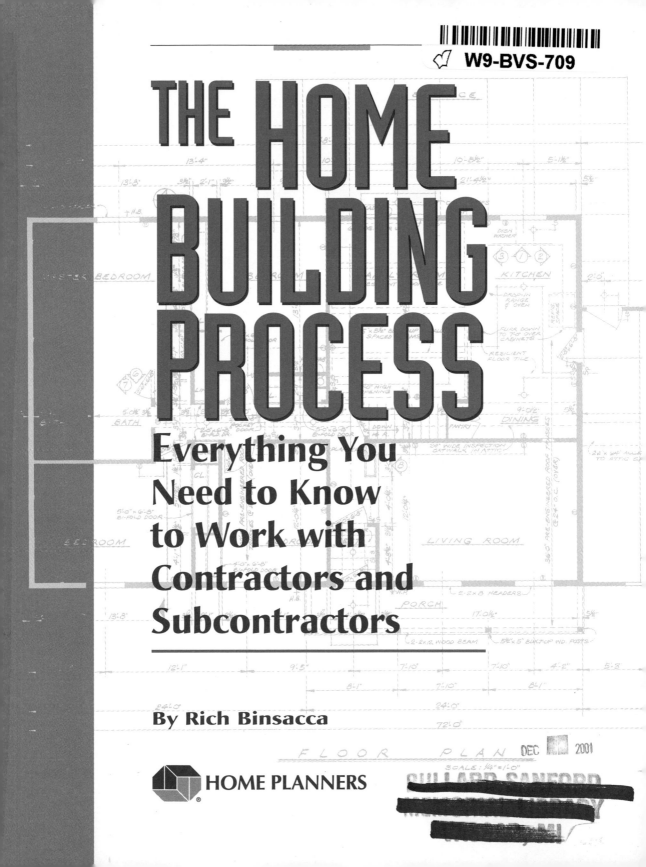

THE HOME BUILDING PROCESS

Everything You Need to Know to Work with Contractors and Subcontractors

By Rich Binsacca

HOME PLANNERS

International Standard Book Number: 1-881955-63-X
Library of Congress Catalog Card Number: 99-72938
Home Planners, LLC, wholly owned by Hanley-Wood, LLC
Tucson, AZ 85741

Book design by Paul Fitzgerald
Cover illustration by Rick Vitullo, AIA.

This book is dedicated to my parents, Bob and Lynn; to my boys, Sam and Nick; and to my friend Rocco Covalt, the best carpenter I ever saw.

This book would not have been possible without the diligent and patient work of Paulette Mulvin, my editor at Home Planners, who supported the concept of this book; and John Shaheen, also of Home Planners, who reviewed the text from a technical perspective and offered expert suggestions to make it accurate and current. Thanks, also, to photographer Kevin Berne, and illustrator/architect Rick Vitullo, AIA, as well as others who supplied photos and graphics.

I used several books for reference, but the most valuable was, without a doubt, the *Means Illustrated Construction Dictionary* compiled by Kornelis Smit and published in 1985. Often, it helped me clarify terms in the text and was a tremendous resource for this book's running glossary. It has for years and always will have a permanent and easy-to-reach place on my desk.

And, of course, I would be remiss not to acknowledge the hundreds of builders, subcontractors, architects, real estate journalists and building products representatives, among others in this industry whom I've interviewed and met over the years. Their insight and enthusiasm have helped me build a body of knowledge and perspective about the home building industry without which the notion, much less the actual production, of this book would have been inconceivable.

Table of Contents

I remember the day I came up with the idea for this book. It was a rainy, windy December day in Belmont, California, a small bedroom community south of San Francisco. I had been invited by my brother-in-law, David, to an NFL playoff game, but first, we stopped by the subdivision where he and my sister Carolyn were having a new home built.

The house had been a frustrating and emotional venture for them already, and it was only in the rough-framing stage. Their builder had long since lost their trust, but the investment potential of the neighborhood, the prospect of a new and bigger house for their growing family, the value of a familiar and safe town and the proximity to both sets of parents and David's law firm made it impossible to turn away from the project at that point. They also had made an emotional investment that perhaps outweighed any practical reasons.

Even at this early stage, they couldn't get the builder to talk to them, and the site superintendent also refused their calls. It was a classic home-building nightmare, one I'd heard about and witnessed countless times as a real estate journalist. They were anxious and nervous about what was happening, why progress seemed so slow, if things were being done correctly and honestly. And there was really no one to answer their questions, except for me when I visited, and a few other people they knew in the architectural and building industry. They were lost and a bit scared.

As we thawed out after the game, I started thinking about what I could do, in my absence from their everyday lives, to help my sister and her husband better understand the process of home building. To explain why builders construct homes in phases (and why their home was one of the last to be completed), and what those weird-looking, I-shaped pieces of lumber were— among the hundreds of questions and concerns they had throughout the ordeal. There must be others like them, I thought, closed off from the process, waiting for their dream homes to be completed by some nameless, faceless builder, hoping it's done right ... and not really knowing what that means.

I knew there were a pile of books written about home building, but I found them written either for people looking to actually build their own homes or for those needing insight into the finer points of designing and financing a custom home. In some cases, the actual process—what happens on the job site—was slight and wedged in between how to hire an architect or builder and what to expect from a builder's customer service department after the sale. Certainly, there was little reference to the dynamic of buying a spec or tract home (that is, from a builder's set of plans in a subdivision) or building from stock plans, despite the fact that a growing percentage of new homes, equaling a half-million or more per year, are built and sold that way across the country.

Obviously, this book is too late for them; their house is completed now and, despite some nagging problems, appears to be well-constructed and sure to last them a long time.

Rather, this book is for the next couple or family who struggles with an uncommunicative builder, a dragging schedule, a floating move-in date and a pile of lumber on their driveway that hasn't been touched by anything but rain in three weeks. Even if they have a good home building experience, are involved in it and feel valued by their builder, these folks hopefully will gain some insight from this book. If it helps them understand how and why homes are built in this country so they can better and more fully enjoy the process, then I've done my job well.

Rich Binsacca

Finding Your Role and Defining Your Responsibilities

Photo: Trus Joist MacMillan

A working relationship with your builder and a solid knowledge of the building process are the keys to a successful project.

Sometime between signing the contract and completion of the house, you lose your identity. You may visit the job site a few times (maybe more, maybe every day), but it's as if the builder is saying, "Thanks for buying a house; I'll call you when it's done." You can see your home taking shape, and the site superintendent does his best to explain what's happening on the days you stop by, but very little appears to be in your control. You don't swing a hammer or sweat pipes, and you've already selected the cabinets and carpeting. At this stage, your part seems ambiguous, if not unnecessary.

Most new home buyers react to this scenario in two ways. Some set up camp at the job site to keep a watchful (if mostly uneducated) eye on what's going on. Others completely shrink away and wait for the phone call telling them it's okay to order the moving van.

Lingo:

site superintendent— the builder's representative during actual construction, in charge of the job site. The superintendent (also called supervisor or foreman) is responsible for managing subcontractors, materials delivery and maintaining the schedule, budget and quality of the project.

sweat pipes—soldering (or connecting with heated lead) metal pipe joints together.

Those who force themselves on their home-building project usually end up dissatisfied: the job went too slow, the place was always a mess, the plumber showed up an hour late, the builder always had an excuse. As a result, the builder's mind set is just to finish the house, bank whatever he can, and move on—except that he's got a month or more to go on the job. At closing, there's a cloud hanging over the project that survives at housewarming parties and, occasionally, in courtrooms.

On the opposite end of the spectrum, home buyers who shy away from the process feel left out. They become detached from something they planned and saved for but aren't allowed (so they think) to watch evolve. They quietly wonder and fret if everything is alright—if the cabinets they want will be the ones installed, if the target date for completion is reliable. When they make a scheduled site visit, they walk around nervously looking for flaws, mistakes or missing pieces, though they aren't quite sure what those might be. As a result, they don't trust themselves to speak up or ask questions, but desperately hope everything will work out by move in.

Obviously, neither choice leaves home buyers especially confident that their new home will be everything they hoped it would. In subdivision (or tract) housing developments, especially, it's difficult to establish enough trust with a builder to find a middle ground where you can feel educated, assured, involved and satisfied in the process.

Finding your role is essential if you are going to truly enjoy your new home from the first day of excavation through the day you unpack, and beyond. Not possible? Sure, there will be days your confidence will wane, when your expectations aren't entirely met. No project is perfect, in home building or any other business. But unless you secure your place in the process at the onset (and there is a place for you), there's little chance of those instances being mere hiccups instead of insurmountable hurdles.

Issues of Control

Defining your role during construction requires a bit of education about the home-building process and builders. This book is designed to help you with the phasing of the process—what happens when, and why—more so than how to build a grade beam or a shear wall. But there are some general issues and circumstances to consider as you develop your identity as the buyer of a new home.

Photo: Trus Joist MacMillan

A builder's main objective is to finish the house on time and according to the plans, which requires tremendous coordination.

A key part of that understanding is knowing what is and is not in the builder's control (and to what extent), and establishing realistic expectations for the work and the schedule.

First, the weather. Builders have big egos, but none big enough to stop a rainstorm or freezing temperatures. It's easy for anyone to understand how bad weather can halt work on a house under construction; what isn't always apparent to a home buyer is how a lost day can trickle down and impact the subcontractors' schedule, delivery and storage of materials and the condition of what's already been built.

INTRODUCTION

The issue with weather is how well prepared the builder is to handle it. There's no real accounting for it, and blaming a builder for bad weather is pointless. However, if he's keeping in touch with his subs and suppliers regarding their availability once the weather clears, making contingency plans to get back on track, and keeping you informed of the process, there's not much more you can ask.

Besides the weather, nothing is truly out of the builder's control. It's just a matter of extent. For instance, builders complain, and rightly so, about the declining availability and quality of skilled labor and reliable materials, such as lumber. But, unlike the weather, these issues are existing conditions of the market or industry, no different than the site's soil content or the local building codes.

Depending on when you purchase your house, you may have the opportunity to tour (or walk through) the home as it is being built, giving you insight into the process and products used.

When the local labor pool may be limited and lacking in skill, for instance, a builder should try to attract and retain the best subcontractors, superintendents and crew members possible by scheduling them properly, providing guidance and paying on time.

Photo: Trus Joist MacMillan

4

Similarly, he may have little to say about whether or when materials are available, but he is responsible for providing enough lead time to a supplier and properly protecting and handling products once they are delivered. And while there may be a backlog at the building department for inspections, savvy builders stay abreast of such circumstances to avoid delays.

Even so, like a co-worker at your office or a vendor you've hired for a project, there's a certain risk associated with relying on other people to complete a job. Housing, perhaps more than any other industry, epitomizes this workplace dynamic.

Know Your Builder

Another good way to figure out where you fit in is to define where you don't. You are not the builder, nor any other tradesperson or subcontractor who might work on the house. You're not a laborer nor a materials supplier. It is not your responsibility to schedule the roofers or even pay them. Seems obvious, right? Tell that to the folks who visit the site every day on their way to work, during their lunch hour and on their way home.

The mystery of home building starts with the builder. Unlock him or her, and you start to demystify the entire process. First, understand and respect that builders are business people. They do what they do essentially for the same reason you specialize in your profession or job: because they can make a living at it and, if they're lucky, enjoy it.

Are builders out to make money? In a word, yes, and there should be nothing wrong with that if it's done honestly. Successful builders develop good business plans, tight production schedules and strong, reliable partnerships—not, as is often the perception, by purposely misordering the kitchen sink, misreading the plans or ignoring phone calls from unpaid suppliers and antsy home buyers.

Most builders are locally based, constructing between one and perhaps a hundred homes a year, depending on the market. Even those that are divisions of larger, national companies operate as members of the local business community. In both cases, builders have invested (sometimes quite heavily) in your community and rely on their local reputation to sell homes and stay in business. Given that investment, it makes no sense to upset a home buyer. Quite simply, some builders just aren't very good at what they do, especially in managing a business or providing customer service. As a result, they end up failing themselves, their company, the job and the customer. It's not a plot. It's life.

Lingo:

lead times—the amount of time between ordering a product or material and when it is delivered.

the trades—subcontractors or specialty contractors, such as electricians, plumbers and painters.

Photo: Rich Binsacca

The "phasing" of new-home developments results in homes in various stages of completion.

Maybe builders get a bad rap, in part, because they are so exposed. Construction is arguably the only industry where the product is literally built in plain view of the customer. Mistakes are more obvious; what's incomplete may appear quite different from what the finished product will look like, yet there's no hiding it. No one sees the trial and error of software development or the creative process of advertising. In almost every other industry, all you see is the finished product.

Some builders embrace this onus and others ignore or neglect it, depending on their business acumen and communication skills. A large builder in Florida, for instance, conducts classes for new and prospective buyers in which they tour homes in various stages of completion to help gain an understanding of the process. This book is designed to provide similar insights.

Other builders are less forthright. They may not see the value or they lack confidence to take such initiative. While the builder in Florida is educating home buyers, he's also planting the seeds of a good local reputation; some builders just don't have vision beyond the house they're building, or maybe even daily tasks.

Remember also, that much of the building process is known and learned, often through generations of home builders and trades-

TAKE NOTE: *Tolerances*

In building, everything is measured and calculated to ensure structural integrity—the depth of the footings, the height of the walls, the squareness of the foundation, the pitch of the roof. Codes, common sense, engineering, experience and basic geometry determine these dimensions. But even with all the high-tech tools and measuring tapes available to builders these days, construction is still an imprecise exercise.

That's where the definition of "tolerance" enters the building vernacular. Tolerance refers to an acceptable, allowable or standard range of precision in various phases of the construction process without sacrificing structural integrity. For instance, it is allowable, according to general industry procedure, for an eight-foot-high wall to be up to 1.5 inches out of plumb; a foundation crack measuring ¼-inch or less in width also passes muster.

For a concerned homeowner, however, a hairline crack or a slightly sloping floor beam—even within industry-proven tolerances—may be unacceptable. Therefore, it's important to discuss with your builder your expectations and his level of tolerance or imprecision and come to an agreement. Quality construction, however hyped, is still relative. Make sure your builder defines it with you.

Lingo:

plumb—exact vertical, typically determined by a plumb bob (a cone-shaped metal weight on the end of a long string).

hairline crack—a thin, slightly visible crack appearing on, but not penetrating the surface.

people. What's different about home building today compared to a hundred years ago is the performance and range of materials and products, not so much the process. Because of their daily exposure to the process and years of experience, builders and contractors

Each stage of construction reveals a bit more of what the finished house will look like.

Photo: Case Corp.

As homes near completion, the number of trade contractors buzzing around the project increases.

Photo: Rich Binsacca

know in the morning what the house will look like by quitting time; it's a day-to-day vision few home buyers can imagine. A disconnect occurs, then, when you take someone who knows his job intimately and mix him with a buying public that has little or no experience with the home-building process. As a consequence, a builder may come across as blasé about a certain phase of construction or concern on your part because he's likely seen it before. That's not to say he shouldn't be responsive, but it may help explain why he's less anxious or concerned than you, the home buyer, who harbors much more anticipation and emotional investment.

Good builders understand that building a house—and especially the mystery of construction—is a big deal to you, a source of anxiety and financial risk. In turn, informed home buyers respect that, to a builder, the process is all in a day's work.

Creating Your Identity

Perhaps the best approach to establishing an identity on the building site is to lead by example, own up to responsibilities and meet people halfway.

The best builders know what you're feeling, your anxieties, ignorance and inexperience with the process. They are well aware of their competition and your ability to select another builder. So they

Depending on your market, a large development could include several builders or just a few (or one) large building companies.

usually bend a little to accommodate your needs by offering or allowing you to make decisions with regard to the exterior appearance of your new home, the appliance package, the lighting, the cabinets, the plumbing fixtures and so on. Some even allow you to move walls, alter staircases or adjust ceiling height—all for the purpose of giving you the house that you want and a level of control in creating something distinctly yours.

With those choices comes responsibility on your part. Builders don't arbitrarily set cut-off dates for certain decisions, such as the color and type of carpeting. Rather, dates are set to accommodate lead times for delivery or the availability of an installer all in an effort to get the job done on time, or at least in a timely manner.

Therefore, you have to respect the schedule and meet the agreed deadlines. When you make a commitment, stick to it; if you want to change it after the deadline, know that it may cost you money or time, maybe both. Such changes often impact the delicate timing of other trades and materials later on in the schedule, as well. Keeping your end of the bargain accomplishes two things: it helps keep the project on track and it shows the builder that you're committed to your promises. Smart builders will return the gesture.

Lingo:

cut-off date—the last day a change can be made or a product ordered without incurring extra cost or delaying construction.

Decisions, Decisions

If you're buying a tract or spec home (that is, a home design already determined by the builder and scheduled for construction), the point at which you enter the home-building process, in large part, determines the decisions you'll be able to make about certain finishes and alterations to the plan.

For instance, if you purchase or put a contract on a house before construction (called a pre-sale), you will often have several choices to make among a limited range of options, including exterior finishes and facade design, appliances and plumbing fixtures, flooring, lighting and wall finishes. It also may be possible to alter the floor plan, enlarging rooms or moving walls to accommodate certain needs.

In addition, you also can often select optional upgrades from the standard offering of products, such as better carpets, doors, roofing and brick instead of clapboard siding, among others. While the choices you have among the range of standard products are included in the listed price of the house, optional upgrades add to the price, although they are amortized (or included) in your mortgage.

If, however, you purchase a house already under construction or perhaps already finished (called standing inventory), your choices are much more limited. It may be, in fact, an "as is" purchase, where nothing can be changed without adding to the price of the house. Occasionally, and especially if the house is still incomplete, you may still be able to select the interior finishes you want from the builder's palette of choices.

To help, most production builders offer model homes and design centers on site, which allow you to see and select your products and finishes at one time upon an approved contract or sale.

Lingo:

planned development—a subdivision or newly constructed neighborhood of homes, starting with an undeveloped or unused section of land.

Every new house needs an inspection card, which remains on site throughout construction.

Photo: Rich Binsacca

Next, come prepared with ideas, wants, needs and concerns right from the start. Be willing to talk about them openly with the builder, even one who may be in the middle of a 200-house phase in a huge planned development. "So many clients are afraid to ask questions because they don't want to look stupid or like they don't know what they're talking about," says one builder, echoing the bulk of the industry.

You've heard it before, but it deserves repeating: There is no such thing as a dumb question. And with that, demand a satisfactory answer; make sure you're comfortable with the explanation or response before letting it go. Then, let it go.

It also helps to study up on the process and learn the lingo. No builder expects you to be an expert, but a little education can go a long way toward building mutual respect. Gaining some insight into the process fosters more and better questions, educated concerns, a keener eye. (To help, please refer to the "Lingo"— or common building terms—explained throughout this book.)

Finally, no matter how shabbily the framing crew is dressed or how rusty the plumber's van, treat the process as a professional undertaking, a for-profit business that requires specialized skill, vision, management and patience. Empathize a little when things hit a snag; put yourself in their position in your job and imagine how it feels in your own job to be let down by a co-worker or delayed by a client's indecision or a system failure. If you expect a builder, or the building process, to be perfect, expect to be disappointed.

Master Filing

Think all subdivision homes these days look alike? There's a reason: master filing. Once the developer sets the codes, covenants and restrictions (CC&Rs) that dictate the design parameters for the entire community, builders submit plans for the homes they want to offer, (usually 3-4, each approved by a design review board) to the building department for compliance with the building code, which regulates health and safety.

Because a builder is likely to construct several of each house design submitted, he applies for a master filing of that plan with the building department to avoid having to go through the code compliance process (also called plan check) every time he sells a given plan. With the master file already approved, the builder simply has to alert the building department that a given house is going to be built on a certain lot in the community, triggering the issuance of a building permit for that house.

Increasingly, to boost sales and create a more diverse streetscape, builders and design review boards are allowing home buyers to either choose from a wider variety of pre-approved finishes and options, or "customize" a tract house within certain parameters. Such changes do not necessarily impact the status of the master filing; in fact, builders are allowed to list potential alterations for a given plan to accommodate aesthetic choices offered to or made by future buyers.

Only in cases where the buyer or the builder decides to change the square footage of the approved house plan (which impacts the value of the structure and thus the cost of the permit), or where changes alter provisions for emergency egress, lighting, ventilation or the structure itself, does the city typically require the builder to refile the revised or new set of plans for building department approval and code compliance.

Lingo:

framing crew—the group of workers hired to build the home's structural frame.

11

If a builder sells homes on speculation (or "on spec"), it's common to see finished homes alongside those just being started.

Photo: Rich Binsacca

By all means, be a part of the process. You have a role and an identity. To what extent and how that relates to your behavior has very much to do with how much time and effort you've put into understanding the building process and your builder. ∎

Site Preparation

Photo: Rich Binsacca

One of the first steps toward completion is grading (or preparing) each homesite out of raw or undeveloped land.

The conditions of raw land in large part determine the finished house. Its soil content, location of the water table and frost line, and natural slope or grade dictate the type of foundation and issues of drainage; its relation to the sun and other elements help shape and refine the home's design, structural frame and orientation—even the location and size of the windows and the choice of exterior finish.

Local or regional codes, materials and building practices also play a part. For instance, clay-laden soils in Indiana often require homes to be built with pier-and-beam foundations (see Chapter 2); exposure from the hot sun in Texas has led to home designs that limit (or even eliminate) windows along the west-facing elevation.

Soils and Survey

The first step in preparing the site for construction is a soils test, a process that takes less than a day to conduct but perhaps a week or more to test in a lab and generate a report. If you're buying a house

Lingo:

water table—the topmost level of ground water or an underground aquifer.

frost line—the depth at which the ground freezes in your area.

Soils test
Approx. time (days): 1
Cum. time (days): 1

Soils report
Approx. time (days): 7
Cum. time (days): 8

Site survey
Approx. time (days): 1
Cum. time (days): 9

in a subdivision, the developer or builder submitted a soils report to the building department as part of the approvals process to begin development. For an individual, undeveloped or rural lot, your builder or perhaps an engineer hired by you will conduct the test. A soils test will provide insight into the porosity of the site and the depth of the topsoil, among other elements. As a result, the engineer, architect or builder will recommend a foundation design and materials to match the soil conditions.

Next is a survey of the lot, which establishes the basic parameters of the home's footprint and location on the site. Like the soils report, a survey may be conducted by a developer of a subdivision or by an agent of the home buyer (such as an engineer), depending on where the house it being built. Ruled by local zoning ordinances that regulate the type and size of a given structure, surveyors must

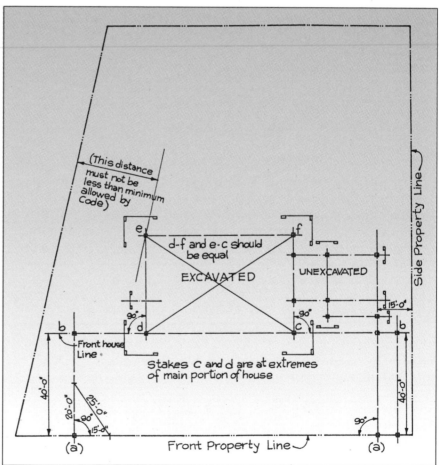

A site survey identifies and confirms the placement of the house on the site.

From: *Dwelling House Construction*

14

Photo: Rich Binsacca

A completed development reflects the surveying and other site work that preceded construction.

be aware of allowable setbacks—the home's distance from houses on neighboring lots.

Surveying a typical residential lot also takes less than a day, with the surveyor using everything from laser-equipped transits to a 100-foot tape measure to stake out the property lines and setbacks to comply with the zoning rules. The survey report also provides a guideline for staking out the dimensions of the site's excavation and eventual foundation.

The survey may also help refine the home's orientation to the sun. Proper orientation is a key consideration, perhaps leading to a slight revision of the plan and its placement on the site to avoid or capture sunlight in certain rooms. It also factors in natural landscape features and other existing conditions before the site is excavated and the building process begins.

Once the survey stakes are set and the orientation established, the contractor—city-approved plans in hand—makes a more refined determination of the home's footprint, or outline of its shape and foundation. With a system of batter boards and taut lines (typically

Foundation staking
Approx. time (days):....1-2
Cum. time (days):....10-11

Lingo:

setbacks—the distance from the property or lot lines to the actual structure (all sides), as determined by local zoning ordinances. Setbacks determine or regulate the space between neighboring homes.

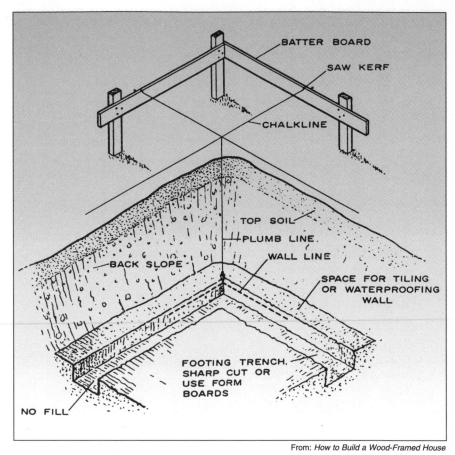

A typical excavation for a house foundation; batter boards help define the edges of the home's "footprint."

From: *How to Build a Wood-Framed House*

heavy-duty string or twine), the builder makes sure the foundation plan is set square on the site and follows the dimensions on the plans. A large house with several corners will likely require several batter boards and crisscrossing taut lines to ensure the foundation is square, so the process can take a day or two to complete.

This system also sets guidelines for the excavator. The batter boards, staked into the ground about two feet or so from the corners of the eventual slab or foundation walls, represent the edges of the trenches the excavator will dig out. These trenches create room for crews to set the footings and foundation wall forms or concrete masonry units (CMUs), also known as concrete blocks. The taut lines, meanwhile, typically indicate the outer edges of the foundation wall or slab and can be used to establish the eventual or estimated height of the foundation walls.

Lingo:

footings—the part or section of the foundation that transfers and spreads the weight of the structure to the soil.

Photo: Rich Binsacca

It may look a little ragged, but the early stages of construction don't have to be neat and tidy.

Don't be overly concerned about upsetting or disturbing the batter boards and taut lines when you visit a staked-out site. Most builders anticipate the likelihood of vandalism, accidents or weather-beaten wear by marking and notching the batter boards with the location of the taut lines they secure. Still, its best to be cautious when you visit the site at this point in the process. Many home buyers, not to mention contractors, have tripped trying to cross taut lines.

This stage gives you the first glimpse of your home, the initial leap from the architect's drawings to the actual building site. Depending on its complexity, the batter boards and taut lines may indicate room dimensions and locations, allowing you to stand in your living room or kitchen and imagine the view from the windows that will be installed a month or so later.

Excavation
Approx. time (days):....2-3
Cum. time (days):....12-14

Excavation

Once the batter boards and taut lines are set and the dimensions and orientation of the foundation checked and confirmed, it's time for the first tangible step toward your home's completion: excavation, which includes the removal of a foot-deep layer of topsoil about 20 feet out from the home's perimeter.

> **TAKE NOTE: Crawlspace excavation**
> For crawlspace foundations (Chapter 2), the excavator may not remove or grade the dirt inside the home's foundation footprint unless it is necessary to promote better drainage or for the placement of a vapor barrier under the house.

Excavation also includes gouging out the foundation trenches or footings, the depth and size of which are determined by the soil conditions and the type of foundation, be it a full basement, crawlspace or slab-on-grade (covered in Chapter 2). Depending on the complexity of the foundation, as well as utility placement and the site itself, excavation can take up to a week. Typically, it's about a two- or three-day process.

Lingo:

vapor barrier—a membrane used to block airborne water (moisture vapor) from entering a space, such as a wall cavity or floor joists. Also called a vapor retarder or moisture barrier.

forms—the moulds into which concrete is poured to form walls, slabs and footings.

drain tiles—a perforated, continuous perimeter pipe that collects and carries water and runoff away from the house to a drainage area (swale, ditch or sewer).

Once a site is graded and staked, excavators dig out trenches for the placement of the foundation formwork.

Photo: Case Corp.

Excavated topsoil is deposited somewhere on or near the lot. It will be reused as the fill dirt, or backfill, and to shape the grade (or slope) of the finished site once the foundation has been poured, the forms stripped away, drain tiles installed and the concrete or CMU mortar joints sufficiently cured and waterproofed.

Occasionally, a builder will "rough-stake" before excavation and then revise or refine the location of his batter boards and taut lines after the site's been dug out and graded. Though it adds a step and maybe an extra day, this process allows for some leeway on the part of the excavator (hardly the most precise craft) and provides assurances for a phase of construction that is perhaps the least easy and most costly to remedy once its done: concrete.

TAKE NOTE: *Natural drainage*

Drainage or runoff is a major concern in new housing developments, especially because so many of today's subdivision lots are cut out and shaped from hillsides and less-than-ideal sites as buildable land becomes more scarce. The result: natural drainage is replaced by the slope of a graded or cut pad and displaced soil, relying on the skill and supervision of the builder and excavator to ensure proper runoff.

To ease your mind a bit, visit the site before it is excavated or cut for the building pad (or lot) to view its natural slope, preferably after a heavy rain or snow melt. You'll see the direction of the runoff and areas of poor drainage, indicating its natural condition and runoff patterns.

Then, go back after the foundation has been back-filled with the site's original topsoil, again after a heavy rainfall, if possible. Within 24 hours, there should be no standing water, but a clear pattern of runoff away from the house and adjacent lots.

Also, be wary if your pad is set lower than those of your neighbors; its a sure bet that water from their gutters, downspouts and finished landscape is likely to end up in your yard unless there is some provision to capture and shed it away. Ideally, the finished lot should lead water away from the property, either to the back and sides and an awaiting swale or concrete V-ditch (which will carry it to a swale or other depository), or to the street and its sewer and drainage system.

Lingo:

cured—dry, as with concrete or mortar.

rough-stake—a preliminary outline of the basic house to direct excavation of the lot or site.

pad—a developed piece of ground, or lot, upon which the house will be built.

swale—a large, gently contoured, often grassy or rock-lined ditch that serves to collect water runoff from several homes in a subdivision.

V-ditch—a small, V-shaped concrete ditch used to collect and carry water runoff from one or two houses to a larger drainage area (a swale or sewer).

stubbed up—pipes or other utility conduits extending from the ground vertically and capped, which will eventually be connected to the home's various energy and water systems.

Finally, before the foundation is formed and set, the builder often installs the underground utility lines that will carry services such as water, sewer and natural gas between the house and the street. The excavator cuts deep, narrow trenches for these pipes and conduits, which are then capped and "stubbed up" above grade for connection later. Occasionally, the trenches and pipes extend through the excavated pad or underneath the eventual slab foundation, depending on where the main service areas of the house are located.

Once the lot is excavated—trenches cut, footings and utility trenches dug out, fill dirt piled high on one side—it can be a real danger zone for anyone not used to walking a building site. Falls into and cave-ins of excavated trenches are among the leading cause of serious injury and death among construction workers. An untrained home buyer is even more vulnerable.

To help mitigate the hazard, excavators typically cut the sides of a foundation trench at a slight angle, away from the excavated work area, and builders try to schedule the foundation or masonry contractor as soon as possible to form and pour the walls or stack the blocks and install the perimeter drain tiles so the trenches can be filled and the threat eliminated. ■

2

Foundations

The depth and extent of excavation depend on the type of the foundation specified for the house.

There are three basic foundation types for residential construction, including slab-on-grade, crawlspace and basement. Each is very different, requires special skill and knowledge to build, and is determined by issues of soil content, site conditions and local housing demand. Despite their differences, these foundation types have three things in common: formwork, footings and anchors.

Footings

Every foundation requires footings—a perimeter slab or sections of poured concrete—to root it to undisturbed soil and to carry and distribute the weight (or load) of the house. Footings also mitigate movement or settling, or at least make such adjustments more uniform across the foundation and frame above.

Form footings
Approx. time (days): 1
Cum. time (days):....13-15

Lingo:

load—the weight of a given component or area of a house.

concrete pour or "the pour"—the process of literally pouring wet concrete into the forms or other mould.

formwork—the moulds into which concrete is poured to form walls, slabs and footings.

set the forms—the process of building and reinforcing the formwork or forms in preparation for concrete.

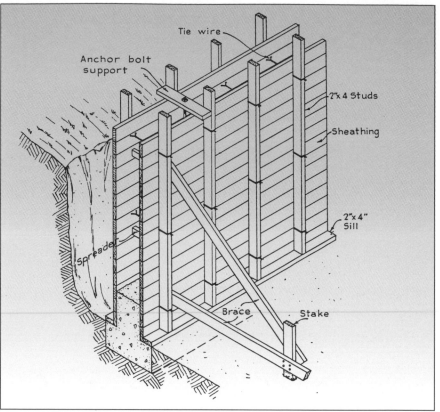

The elements of a typical poured concrete foundation wall for a full basement. In this case, the footing is simply formed by excavated dirt.

From: *Dwelling House Construction*

TAKE NOTE: Footings

It's a myth that footings are somehow connected to or resting on bedrock; such engineering is usually reserved for dams, not dwellings. Footings, however, are usually made wider than the thickness of the foundation walls set upon them. Their exact dimensions are determined by the load above, soil content and other factors germane to the site.

Pour footing

Approx. time (days): 1
Cum. time (days):....14-16

In addition to loads and soil conditions, the depth and dimension of the footings also depend on the existence of a frost line (the greatest depth at which frost penetrates the earth) and the water table. Footings must extend about a foot or more below the frost line and must avoid the water table, both of which can put extreme pressure on the concrete. Either condition may dictate a different foundation than the one originally planned, such as a slab-on-grade instead of a full basement.

All footings are constructed of poured concrete and are usually reinforced with steel bars (or rebar). Reinforcement helps the house better resist movement and failure under extreme conditions, including earthquakes and floods. Once excavated, the footings may be formed, or moulded, with lumber and stakes for the concrete pour. In some cases, the excavated hole serves as an adequate form, with the concrete poured directly into the ground. Such differences depend on local building practices and codes. Forming and pouring the footings takes a day or two, with the actual pour done in a few hours.

Form foundation
Approx. time (days): 1
Cum. time (days):....15-19

> **TAKE NOTE: Other footings**
> Footings also are typically required for peripheral elements, like chimneys, partitions, columns and other localized loads.

Once a concrete pour starts, the pace is fast and furious to ensure proper and even curing of the concrete.

Photo: Portland Cement Assn.

23

Formwork

Once the footings are formed (in some cases, even poured and set, with rebar or anchor bolts embedded in them to tie into the wall above), formwork for the foundation walls, grade beams or slab begins. Again, formwork is simply the mould into which the concrete will be poured to create the walls, floor slab or beams that will support the home's frame, depending on the type of foundation. On most jobs, it takes about two days to set the forms and prepare them for concrete.

Formwork is rarely pretty. In single-family housing construction (as opposed to larger and taller non-residential buildings), formwork for grade beams and slabs is typically a series of old 2-by-6 boards staked in place and strapped across the top to create what looks like a trellis for a model train. For slab foundations, the forms are set only on one side, indicating the edges of the foundation.

For the walls of a full basement, the forms arrive in panels measuring about the size of a sheet of plywood (4x8 feet). To create the mould of a 4-inch-wide wall, the forms are set facing each other and connected by wires, ties and clamps. Both sides of the formed wall are then braced by pieces of 2-by and 4-by lumber nailed to the forms. Spreaders and wire ties set across the top of the forms (and at strategic places between them along the height of the wall) keep the forms at a consistent and uniform width to accept the concrete. Once the forms are removed, the interior ties are cut flush against the resulting wall and patched.

No matter the foundation type, forms can appear ragged and near collapse to someone seeing them in place for the first time. While forms need to be of sufficient quality to withstand the forces of poured and curing concrete (and are often inspected to ensure their strength), they also are often used and reused on several jobs before being retired as scrap lumber or waste. Their appearance, however poor, does not affect the structural integrity of the poured concrete.

As reused equipment, forms are removed (or stripped) from the concrete once it has begun to set (from a few days to a week or more). Stripping can cause some careless gouging of the forms during the removal of fasteners, bracing and ties—resulting in a ragged, if not completely damaged, material.

The only time you might not see formwork is if the builder chooses to excavate the mould out of the site (typically reserved, if at all, for

Lingo:

grade beams—structural members made of poured concrete that connect and reinforce structural piers.

flush—a surface that is flat or even with an adjoining surface.

single-family housing—a structure or dwelling unit built for one family, as opposed to an apartment building or duplex.

scrap lumber—small sections of lumber cut from longer members during construction, often used in non-structural or support applications.

stripping forms—the process of removing the forms from the poured concrete after sufficient curing (or drying).

bracing—a temporary support for aligning and supporting vertical concrete forms (for walls).

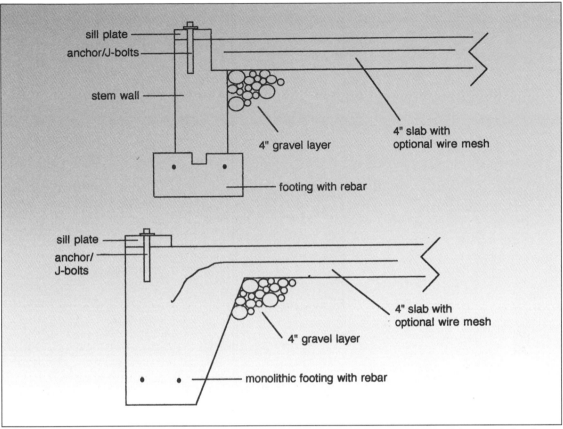

Rich Binsacca

Slab-on-grade foundations, either monolithic (below) or with separate wall and footings or beams (above) are used on nearly half of all new homes.

slab-on-grade jobs), or use concrete blocks, or CMUs, to build the basement walls.

Anchors

Lastly, every basement type requires a provision for anchoring it to the house frame above. Typically, a series of anchor bolts (or J-bolts, so-called because of their shape) are embedded into the wet concrete immediately after it is poured. These bolts, set about eight inches apart or as specified on the foundation plan, extend high enough above the top of the foundation to accommodate a 1½-inch-thick piece of lumber (called a sill plate). The anchor bolts are threaded on the exposed end to receive a nut that secures the sill to the foundation at strategic points.

These bolts, among other attachments and straps discussed later, provide a continuous load path from the weight and design of the frame through the foundation to the footings.

Lingo:

continuous load path—the integration of structural components so that loads are transferred from the frame to the foundation and soil.

Photo: Rich Binsacca

During excavation and foundation work, basic utilities are run to the house from the street and "stubbed up" for connection later.

TAKE NOTE

Lingo:

settling—when sections of pavement or structures drop (or lower in elevation) because of their mass, weight imposed on them, or displacement of their support (typically soil).

subsurface drainage—the drainage of water, either natural or imposed, below the surface of the ground.

TAKE NOTE: Curing concrete

Concrete begins to cure after just a few hours (slower when it's cold, faster in hot temperatures), after which it should not be disturbed; in fact, after reaching its initial curing stage, concrete will not chemically bond to newly poured concrete adjacent to it. After about eight hours, concrete reaches its "final set" stage.

Because concrete is a quick-drying material, the actual pouring of concrete is a chaotic, frenetic and sloppy process no matter the foundation type. It lasts perhaps an hour, and includes tamping and vibrating the wet concrete to fill any voids and even its content throughout the forms. Finishing chores, such as smoothing the slab, cutting control joints and setting anchor bolts, occurs for a few hours, at most, after the pour.

Foundation Types

Nationwide, about half of all new homes are built on a slab foundation while the other half have crawlspaces or full basements. At the local level, however, it's rare to see much deviation among new

26

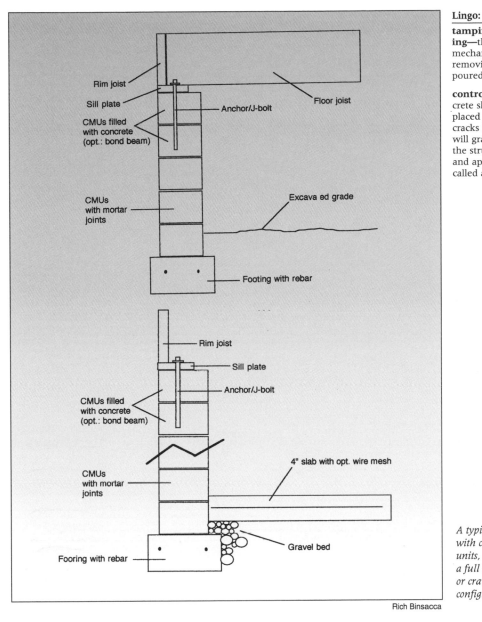

Rim joist

Sill plate

CMUs filled
with concrete
(opt.: bond beam)

Anchor/J-bolt

Floor joist

CMUs
with mortar
joints

Excava ed grade

Footing with rebar

Rim joist

Sill plate

Anchor/J-bolt

CMUs filled
with concrete
(opt.: bond beam)

4" slab with opt. wire mesh

CMUs
with mortar
joints

Gravel bed

Fooring with rebar

Rich Binsacca

A typical foundation built with concrete masonry units, or CMUs, either as a full basement (below) or crawlspace (above) configuration.

homes—the majority, for reasons of soil content, the local building culture, codes, and buyer expectations and demand, have the same type of foundation.

Slab-on-grade

Slab foundations are common in areas of expansive soil, where a high clay content causes problems with settling and inadequate sub-

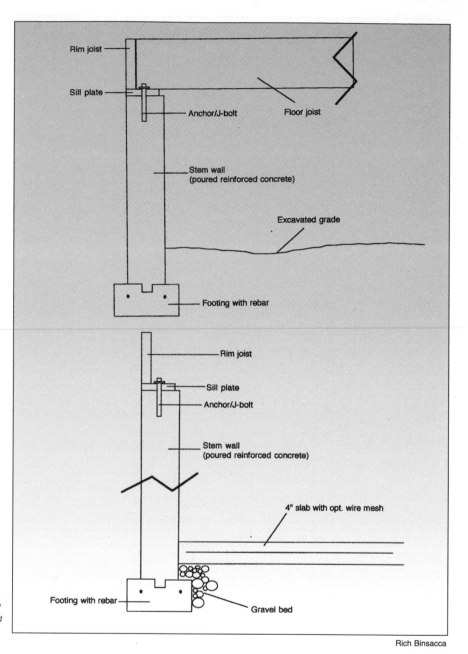

Rim joist

Sill plate

Anchor/J-bolt

Floor joist

Stem wall
(poured reinforced concrete)

Excavated grade

Footing with rebar

Rim joist

Sill plate

Anchor/J-bolt

Stem wall
(poured reinforced concrete)

4" slab with opt. wire mesh

Footing with rebar

Gravel bed

Rich Binsacca

Most full-basement foundations are built with separate footings and walls to ensure the integrity of each structural component.

Lingo:

monolithic slab—a section of concrete created in a single pour or cast, with no joints other than control joints.

surface drainage; they also became popular once technology evolved away from coal-fired furnaces to smaller electric and natural gas equipment, thus eliminating the primary need for a basement (that is, for coal storage). And with the three-car garages and walk-in closets of today's housing, a musty, damp basement seems inadequate—even unnecessary—for storage of anything.

Slabs also are easier, faster and cheaper to build than full basements, requiring a day or less to form and prepare for concrete once excavation has been completed. Most affordable or first-time-buyer homes are on slabs to lessen construction costs and thus the price of the finished house. They require less excavation and formwork and are often poured at the same time as their footings to create a monolithic structure.

Slab foundations rest on a bed of washed gravel to facilitate drainage under the slab and occasionally contain pipes or conduits for various utilities that will be set within the concrete. Measuring between six- and eight-inches thick, slabs also are often reinforced with rebar along the perimeter and a thick wire mesh across the breadth. All slabs are finished with control (or expansion) joints—man-made grooves along the surface of the slab to attract and regulate cracking that will occur during the curing process.

Crawlspaces
Why would anyone go to the trouble of excavating for footings and forming walls if it only resulted in an unusable, two-foot-high, spider-infested space under the house? Several reasons, including easier access to service pipes and conduits under the floor. Crawlspaces also allow for a wood-framed floor just above the graded lot (instead of a hard, cold slab), which gives you more floor finish options. Finally, this type of foundation accommodates soil, drainage and climate conditions that might result in excessive moisture build-up on a slab or full basement, or that require a deeper footing than a typical slab might provide.

Crawlspace foundations require about twice as much formwork as a slab (two sides instead of one), and necessitate a provision for poured or block walls (called stem walls) extended up from the footings along the perimeter of the foundation. Thus, it may take a full day or more to complete the formwork for a crawlspace.

Lingo:

washed gravel—small rocks that have been cleaned of dirt and other debris, typically used as a drainage medium under dirt and concrete.

wire mesh—lengths of heavy-gauge wire welded into a square-crossing mat and used to reinforce concrete slabs.

TAKE NOTE: Efflorescence
Do you notice white, chalky stuff on your basement wall or slab foundation? Its called efflorescence—salt deposits from the moisture evaporating out of the concrete or mortar as it cures. Don't worry; it's normal. After a week or so, hose or lightly scrub it off and forget about it.

Lingo:

stem walls—foundation or other concrete or masonry walls resting on a continuous footing and extending only a few feet above grade.

A completed grade beam and slab also include embedded bolts and metal straps for connection to the structural framing, as well as elements such as foundation vents.

But unlike a slab and certainly a full basement design, the interior of a crawlspace foundation's perimeter walls can often be left unexcavated. Only in cases where a vapor or moisture barrier is to be installed, or where a particular drainage pattern needs to be manicured, is grading required. Finally, a crawlspace foundation requires the least amount of concrete (depending on the depth of the walls and footings) among the three foundation options.

An alternative to the typical footing and perimeter stem-wall design of most crawlspace foundations is a system of piers and grade

Photo: Rich Binsacca

beams. If codes or soil conditions require deep footings for a crawl-space, the contractor and architect may decide to drill a series of holes (the dimensions of which are determined by engineering calculations) to the desired depth.

Then, caissons—tubular cages of steel rebar designed to reinforce the concrete—are dropped into the holes, with rebar extended up above grade and bent in several directions to tie into the grade beams that connect the piers. The resulting beams are formed as stem walls for the frame above, as with a conventional crawlspace foundation.

Like a slab, a pier-and-beam foundation is poured all at once, with anchor bolts inserted into the grade beams immediately after the pour. Once the concrete is sufficiently poured and the forms stripped away, the builder or framing crew can move in to install the sill plate and start framing the floor and walls.

TAKE NOTE: *Full-height basements*

The typical dimensions of form panels and other foundation form materials often result in a basement ceiling height of less than eight feet. But today, with improved waterproofing components and the demand for more living space, home buyers may want a little more clearance if they want to use the below-grade space for an extra bedroom or family room. If you want a full basement with ceiling height to match (at least nine feet), make sure the builder plans for it.

Full Basements

Up until about the 1930s, basements were a necessary evil in our nation's home-building history. Dark and damp, they housed the heating equipment and the pile of coal it required. They also served, in some cases, as cold storage for perishable foods. The basement was not at all, as one might imagine today, livable space. Today, however, advances in below-grade waterproofing and other products and structural systems—not to mention the scarcity of buildable land and a propensity of smaller housing lots—have allowed some builders to market basements as livable, light-filled space.

Due in many respects to its construction, a full basement is simply a deeper crawlspace; yet, finished with a poured concrete floor, it also resembles a below-grade slab. In building a full basement, the contractor may pour the footings (and perhaps the slab, as well) before the full-height walls, if only to ensure that the concrete in these critical areas sufficiently fills its formwork. Builders who pour the

Pour foundation /set CMUs
Approx. time (days):....1-2
Cum. time (days):....16-21

Lingo:

grade—ground level, either natural or cut.

Insulated Concrete Forms

They may never take over the building world, but insulated concrete forms (ICFs) offer builders—and home buyers—some intriguing advantages as formwork for poured concrete walls, both below and above grade.

ICFs are made from rigid foam similar to an old-fashioned ice chest. The foam is either shaped into preformed blocks, like long, lightweight CMUs, or arrives in large panels that are connected similarly to standard form panels. Set directly on the footings, ICFs form the wall for a concrete pour, complete with interior rebar, beam pockets, empty utility conduits and window and door bucks.

The difference is that these forms stay put. Though they have no structural value, ICFs offer significant insulating value and basic moisture protection; they also save the builder time because there's no formwork to remove and store for the next job.

They're also extremely lightweight, allowing faster installation before the concrete pour.

The problem is, they look weird, especially when they are used to form the above-

ground walls of the house in addition to the foundation. Though a relatively new technology to U.S. home building, ICFs (in one form or another) have been used in Europe since the '40s. Builders who've taken the leap to use them in the States swear by them, and homeowners enjoy not only a permanently insulated structure, but impressive noise reduction value, as well.

walls, slab and footings at the same time use mechanical vibrators and tamping equipment to move the concrete into place.

Of the three basic types of residential foundations, full basements also require the most work, from excavation of a deep crater to tall, two-sided form panels, hundreds of tie wires, and yards of rebar set within the panels. As a result, forming a full-height basement can be a two- or three-day job.

There's also a sufficient risk from working both below grade and high above the excavated hole. Full basements require more concrete and also more time to form the walls and to let them cure before framing begins—the latter perhaps up to a week or more depending on the outside temperature.

And even though some contractors may employ a mason to stack CMUs for the full-height basement walls, that method is laborious, often requires the insertion of rebar and other stabilizers, and takes just as long for the mortar between the blocks to cure as it does for a poured wall to cure. In

Photo: James F. Wilson

A crane and a boom are necessary equipment to reach above-grade concrete walls during a pour.

fact, builders may only use block walls if the plans call for it, typically when the interior walls of the basement are to be left exposed.

Depending on the design—specifically if windows or doors (from a walkout or hillside lot) are to be installed in the basement walls—the forms will be interrupted by a variety of other components and cut-outs.

For instance, you may see a few sections of plastic pipe inserted through the form panels to accommodate the installation of utility and other service lines after the concrete is poured. Window

Lingo:

mason—a person trained to work with masonry, including brick and concrete block (CMUs)

brick or stone veneer—thin pieces of natural or synthetic stone or brick material fastened to a wall or walkway to simulate full-size pieces.

bucks—cut-outs framed in structural lumber—provide a space and a nailing surface for window and door installation. Beam pockets, typically cut into the inside face of the forms and wrapped in black building paper, form ledges for structural beams to support the frame above; a small ledge formed along the outside face of the panels near or just above grade level provides sufficient space for brick or stone veneer on the outside of the house.

Foundation /motar cure; strip forms

Approx. time (days):....3-7

Cum. time (days):....19-28

While setting forms for a typical, 1,500-square-foot house takes a day or so (sped along by the use of pre-assembled form panels), these intrusions and accommodations may add another day before the builder can schedule the actual concrete pour. Then, the trucks roll in, usually equipped with a extendible arm and long hose, called a boom, that allows workers to more easily direct the concrete into the forms and around window and door bucks while the mixer is parked at the curb.

> ### TAKE NOTE: Concrete and climate
>
> In extreme temperatures, hot or cold, concrete can be poured and cured properly, but it requires more care and a bit of creativity. In hot climates, concrete is in danger of curing too fast and unevenly, leaving cracks bigger than tolerances allow. To compensate, builders and their crews will keep the surfaces of the concrete wet, typically with just a simple garden hose. In cold climates, ready-mix companies will occasionally use hot water as they mix the concrete; other methods to speed the curing process—which simply allows the job to stay on schedule—include blankets, straw and portable heaters.

Stripping forms. After as few as three days, the forms can be stripped away and re-stacked, leaving somewhat smooth walls with wires sticking out of them, perhaps a few honeycomb-looking patches where the concrete wasn't tamped down properly, and J-bolts extending from the top, ready to accept the sill plate.

Basement waterproofing

Approx. time (days): 1

Cum. time (days):....20-29

Patching the wall, especially to cover honeycombs and cut tie wires, is a standard procedure requiring a chemically compatible mastic. The result is a smoother surface, which will better adhere to the waterproofing membrane desired for most of today's basements.

Waterproofing. In fact, as home buyers increasingly want below-grade livable space for a home office, family room or apartment, builders have come to rely on spray-applied waterproofing membranes and insulation panels to block moisture, maintain a more even temperature and resist water pressure and penetration against the foundation walls.

Lingo:

pre-assembled form panels—formwork built elsewhere and delivered to the job site for erection.

ready-mix—wet or "plastic" concrete manufactured for delivery; a mixture of cement sand, and water.

honeycomb—a rough, pitted surface resulting from incomplete filling of concrete in the forms or inadequate tamping and vibrating.

spray-applied waterproofing—a polymer-enhanced membrane applied to a concrete surface through an air-driven hose and spray nozzle.

condensation—the conversion of moisture vapor to water.

A worker directs the boom hose to fill the cavities of the foundation or above-grade wall formwork.

Photo: James F. Wilson

Remarkably, trained waterproofing crews can start working within hours after the forms are removed; many provide patching and other preparation services to assure their product adheres to the outside foundation walls. Once the surfaces are prepped, it takes perhaps an hour to apply a .6-millimeter-thick membrane, either a non-flammable asphalt polymer or a solvent-based rubber.

TAKE NOTE: Basement waterproofing

Waterproofing or dampproofing? There is a difference. Until improved technology and competitive pricing made waterproofing systems affordable for home builders, many (along with their home buyers) thought they were providing adequate below-grade moisture protection by dampproofing—an black asphalt system akin to hot-mopping the roof of a warehouse. While dampproofing retards water and moisture, it weakens under pressure and time, eventually falling away from the wall. If you plan to use your basement as a living space, complete with carpet and wallpaper, insist the builder install a waterproofing system.

Photo: Koch Waterproofing Systems

The excavated foundation trenches come in handy when applying below-grade foundation waterproofing materials, the last step before backfilling the walls.

Waterproofing membranes dry very quickly, within an hour of application, which allows the crew to begin installing thin, foam or fiber glass panels to protect the membrane from backfill debris, insulate the concrete to reduce indoor condensation, and help shed away any water that might get between the panels and the wall.

Perimeter drainage
Approx. time (days):....1-2
Cum. time (days):....21-31

Perimeter Drainage

Before the excavator returns to backfill the trench and groom the grade for proper drainage, there's one more step: the perimeter drainage system. Long, perforated plastic pipes, set at or just below the top of the footings on a sloping bed of gravel, serve to carry water away from the foundation and out to a swale or other depository. The pipes are protected from dirt clogging their function by another layer of gravel on top, which filters away dirt and debris. Some installers also set a thin, tightly woven nylon mesh over the top of the pipe for the same reason, in addition to the gravel.

This system of connected pipes, all sloping to the lowest point of the excavated lot and the site's natural drainage pattern, is often called a French drain or drain tiles. Think of it as an underground gutter system.

With gravel protecting the perimeter drain and the waterproofing system in place (a job that takes a day or two), the excavator can come back to the site and, using the topsoil he removed a week or two before, fill the trenches and any other areas to within about eight inches of the top of the foundation wall. Leaving some of the wall exposed and clear of the fill keeps ground water and moisture from edging up to the wood frame components of the house—a much more permeable and vulnerable material than concrete. ■

Photo: Case Corp

Final grading of the site is a key element in promoting proper drainage away from the house.

Lingo:

ground water—an underground source of water; an aquifer (as opposed to surface water, such as a reservoir).

3

Framing

Photo: Trus Joist MacMillan

Framing materials are often delivered in stages to mitigate waste and on-site theft.

More than any other phase of home construction, framing is the most dramatic. During this stage, progress seems faster and more noticeable on a daily basis. Within a few weeks, your house unfolds from scaled-down, two-dimensional floor plans to a three-dimensional, full-scale model that you can walk through and touch.

A popular analogy is to liken a home's frame to a human skeleton; that is, interconnected parts forming a basic structure for various other systems and a substrate for a protective skin.

But a home's frame (like your own skeletal system) is much more than a structural entity. In fact, its design and construction in large part determine, both directly and indirectly, the overall performance of the house—its insulating value, whether the floors squeak or bounce, the operation of the windows and doors and the home's

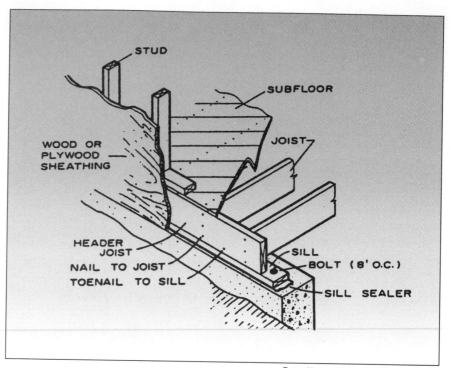

The basic elements of a raised-floor system for a platform frame, including the connection of the structural frame to the foundation.

From: *How to Build a Wood-Framed House*

resistance to wind and weather, among several others discussed later.

Despite dramatic progress, the framing stage often ebbs and flows. Some days or weeks, you'll see walls rise up and roof trusses installed, giving the impression that construction is moving quickly. Other days, while the site superintendent juggles the electrician and the plumber amid the next scheduled delivery of materials and a shorthanded framing crew, progress appears to slow down.

Timing during this stage is critical, as is close attention to detail and the management of various subtrades and materials suppliers. If the plumber is running late or if materials aren't delivered on time, the entire schedule can get thrown out of whack.

In fact, if everything ran perfectly, a typical new house could conceivably be framed, roughed-in with all the necessary mechanical systems and sheathed within about two weeks—maybe less with pre-built components. In the real world, it generally takes about twice that time, perhaps more if there are delays due to bad weather, inadequate or poor-quality materials, labor shortages or unavailable subcontractors.

Lingo:

roof trusses—pre-assembled sections that form the shape and structure of the roof.

40

Photo: Trus Joist MacMillan

In production or "tract" home development, homes are often framed in a matter of a few days, and proper scheduling of materials deliveries becomes critical.

The Platform Frame

The prevailing method for building modern homes is called platform framing. Essentially, each level of the house, from the foundation up, is a separate structure built on a platform. But even that definition is a bit of a misnomer. Each level, in fact, is engineered and built with the other structural entities and subsequent platforms in mind, creating an interconnected system.

For homes with a basement or crawlspace foundation, the first platform—typically built from wood components—is constructed over the foundation footprint; for slab-on-grade homes, the concrete slab itself serves as the first platform.

TAKE NOTE: Rough framing

House framing is often called rough framing, or rough carpentry. These terms allude to the fact that the structural members will be hidden from view when the home is finished, and thus don't require as much care or thought with regard to appearance as opposed to structural accuracy. In addition, rough-frame carpentry is less precise than applying door casings, baseboard trim or other interior and exterior finishes. Still, quality carpenters and framing contractors are just as skilled as those who apply the finishing touches.

TAKE NOTE

41

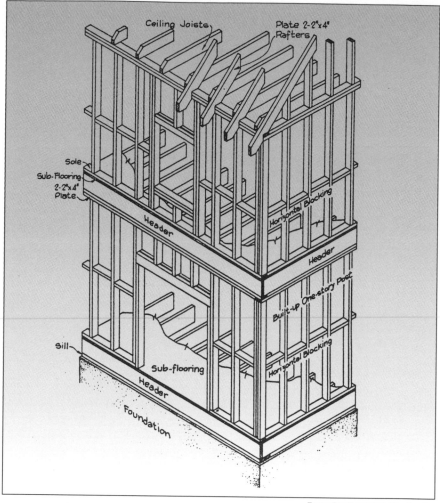

Ceiling Joists

Plate 2-2"x4"
Rafters

Sole

Sub-Flooring

2-2"x4"
Plate

Horizontal Blocking

Header

Header

Built-up One-story Post

Sill

Sub-flooring

Horizontal Blocking

Header

Foundation

*The basic elements of a
modern platform frame.*

From: *Dwelling House Construction*

The Sill Plate

In either case, the first component of a house frame is the sill, or sole, plate. A 2-by wood member is laid flat on the wall or slab and drilled with holes to accommodate the anchor (or J-) bolts protruding from the foundation walls or slab. The sill is installed around the perimeter of the foundation (outlining the footprint), as well as on all interior grade beams or other concrete components that will come in contact with the frame. This bolted connection ties the frame to the foundation.

Because the sill plate is made of wood and comes in direct contact with concrete, building codes require that it be treated with a rot-resistant preservative, often giving the wood a greenish or dark

Lingo:

2-by/4-by—the nominal size, in inches, of the narrow plane of standard wood framing components, as in a 2-by-4.

brown tint. The preservative is injected by intense heat and pressure at the lumber mill or factory. Its purpose is to inhibit the migration of moisture from the ground and the foundation to the untreated wood frame.

The sill also allows the builder or framing contractor an opportunity to adjust a foundation wall or slab that is slightly out of level by "shimming" the sill plate.

Shimming involves inserting thin, tapered strips of wood or metal under the sill plate before securing the plate to the anchor bolts. Otherwise, if the house is framed with a slope or crown (a slight bump) at the sill, certain parts of the house can become chronic trouble spots: windows that are hard to open, sloping floors, doors that won't stay open or properly close.

Regardless of the foundation's condition, the builder or framing contractor should always start with a level sill plate.

TAKE NOTE: *Value-engineering*

Over the years, building codes have been altered to allow the elimination of some framing components, including the sill plate, deemed unnecessary in certain situations. The thinking is that by eliminating these pieces without affecting the overall integrity of the structure, builders (and thus, home buyers) can save money.

In fact, most builders and framing contractors are either unaware of the altered building codes or unwilling to eliminate the sill plate or any other structural component in traditional platform frame construction. Many consider the potential cost savings insignificant; others question the resulting quality and stability of the structure. Even local code officials and building inspectors are hesitant to concede these "value-engineering" measures, despite allowances in the code. When presented with such specifications, officials scrutinize the plans and spend extra time during inspections to ensure that minimum structural standards are met.

The Floor System

For a house with a basement or crawlspace, the next step is the installation of the floor beams and joists, which provide the underlying structure of the first platform.

If the crawlspace is simply exposed dirt, the builder may install a continuous layer of thick plastic sheeting, called visquine, before the installation of the joists. The plastic layer prevents the soil's mois-

Lingo:

floor joists—framing components that create the structure of the floor.

value-engineering—the process of evaluating the cost and structural value of a product or material to the overall structure.

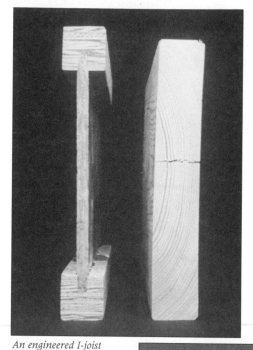

ture vapor from condensing on the floor joists above. This condensation can result in moisture damage to the floor structure, causing a variety of problems such as dry rot and mold, squeaks, warping and even damage to the finished floor material.

Depending on the dimensions of the foundation, a large beam—typically of solid wood, but occasionally of heavy-gauge steel—may be installed in the beam pocket or rested on top of the foundation walls. Such beams provide intermediate support for the floor joists to limit their deflection (or bounce) as the joists span across the foundation. In some cases, the joists may simply span over the top of the beam for support; in other cases, the beam may intersect the joists, which are then nailed to the sides of the beam. Both methods provide similar stability.

An engineered I-joist (left), so-called because of its profile, eliminates the effects of shrinkage experienced by traditional, 2-by framing materials (right).

Right: New materials, such as engineered wood I-joists for flooring structures, help create stronger and more reliable homes.

Photos: Trus Joist MacMillan

There are times when such intermediate (or "carrying") beams are unnecessary. Some joists, especially those constructed of engineered wood materials (so-called I-joists because of their shape) may be strong enough to span across the foundation without support and without risk of unacceptable deflection along their length.

Beams may also be eliminated if concrete grade beams or piers are built during the foundation stage to intersect or carry the joists from below, or if the length from one side of the foundation to the other is short enough for a standard 2x10 or 2x12 to adequately span without support.

TAKE NOTE: *Joist spans*

How long is too long when it comes to the span capability of a floor joist? Like all framing components, floor joists are rated for their span and load capability depending on the type of material (with wood, the tree species; with steel, the gauge) and their dimension (length, depth and width) for a given situation. The rating includes how much weight will be placed upon the joists when the home is occupied.

These ratings are published by trade associations and individual manufacturers in the form of span and load tables or charts, which serve to guide builders, engineers and architects in designing the home's frame. The calculations are then checked and confirmed by the building department during the permit process to ensure safety and minimum structural integrity.

One thing to look out for: Production or tract-home builders will often specify the minimum-sized joists; that is, the joist size that provides the least capability (and thus, the lowest cost) while still meeting code. The result may be a floor that is somewhat bouncy, even though the joists are rated for that span. If you're building a custom home or have an opportunity to express your expectations about deflection to the builder before your home is built, he or she can specify higher-rated joists to meet your definition of quality and mitigate deflection.

The joists, typically 2x10s, 2x12s or engineered I-joists of comparable dimension, are laid out across the foundation about 16 inches apart. In some instances, depending on the capability of the joists and the engineering of the floor frame, they may be spaced wider, perhaps up to two feet.

The joists are secured to the foundation walls at the sill plate, typically with a few nails. A rim joist is then nailed to the exposed ends of the joists along the foundation perimeter, enclosing the platform frame and stabilizing the joists.

Engineered wood I-joists require no crowning; by design, they create a flat, even floor frame.

Photo: Trus Joist MacMillan

Occasionally, some builders or framers will install mid-span blocking—sections of wood nailed between the joists, sometimes diagonally—in an effort to make the floor even stiffer. Mid-span blocking was once code-mandated, but is now optional because it is inconclusive whether the blocks actually stiffen the floor. If you don't see mid-span blocks, don't worry.

Floor Sheathing

The last piece of the first-floor platform is the sheathing—usually 4x8-foot, ¾-inch-thick panels made of plywood or oriented strand board (OSB) laid on top of the joists and either nailed or screwed into the floor structure. The result is the first-floor platform, often called a "raised-floor platform" when built over a basement or crawlspace.

On occasion, and sometimes depending on local building codes or the framing specifications, a continuous layer (or bead) of gooey adhesive is placed along the top edge of each joist, end to end,

Lingo:

bead—a continuous, half-round line of caulking material used to create a barrier between two materials or products, such as a window in a rough frame opening.

Photo: Trus Joist MacMillan

Joist hangers, among other metal connectors, hold joists and other framing members in place and also add stability in adverse weather or earthquakes.

immediately before the panels are laid down and fastened. The panels press down on the bead of adhesive to secure their bond with the joists.

TAKE NOTE: Crowning

Standard 2-by wood joists are often delivered with a slight, natural curvature (or crown) from one end to the other along their narrow edge. As such, builders and framers install joists with the crowns facing up, giving the entire floor structure a slight, rounded bump in the middle. By "crowning" the floor joists, the framer knows that once the subfloor sheathing panels are installed over the joists and more weight is applied from additional framing members above, the crowns (and thus, the entire floor) will flatten and become level. Failure to crown the joists, however (installing some up and others down), can result in an uneven platform. Installing the joists crown-down will cause a sag.

Engineered I-joists, in contrast to standard milled lumber, are constructed without a crown; rather, they are manufactured to be perfectly straight along all edges. Thus, framers and their work crews don't have to concern themselves with crowing when they install I-joists, one of several reasons builders use these engineered framing components.

Lingo:

crown—a natural curvature along the length of a section of wood. In concrete, a crown may be moulded on purpose to shed water away from the surface.

subfloor sheathing—panels of plywood used on top of the floor joists to stabilize and enclose the floor structure, creating a flat platform.

Walls are often constructed on the deck or platform, then raised into position.

Photo: Trus Joist MacMillan

Raised-floor platform
Approx. time (days): 3
Cum. time (days):....24-34

Lingo:

shrinkage—the contraction of a material due to moisture, cold or other climate condition.

This bond provides added protection against floor squeaks, which most often occur when the sheathing separates from the joists because of moisture or shrinkage of one or both framing members. The squeak you hear is most often a sheathing panel rubbing against the length of a nail that is no longer holding tight to the joist; hence, quality-conscious builders use screws instead of nails and glue the subfloor to the joists to eliminate squeaks.

Depending on the size and shape of the foundation footprint, constructing the first-floor platform over a basement or crawlspace takes about three days (for slab-on-grade homes, the mere installation and shimming of the perimeter sill plate secured to the anchor bolts takes but a few hours). At this point, the only noticeable difference is that the basement has been covered up, with perhaps a hole cut (or simply outlined) in the platform for an eventual staircase to the lower level. But the stage is set—literally—for some dramatic progress.

Wall Framing

The next time you stop by the job site after the floor sheathing is installed, you'll probably see some, if not all, of the walls for the first floor in place, braced by 2x4s set diagonally on either side of each wall section. The basic wall section consists of three parts: a horizontal plate at the bottom (for slab homes, the pressure-treated sill plate serves this purpose), the vertical studs and another horizontal plate at the top.

Some sections may feature a window or door cut-out, typically requiring a larger horizontal member above the opening, called a header. The top plate may also be doubled to accommodate additional weight from above or to achieve the desired ceiling height.

Smaller vertical members, such as under a window opening, are called "cripple" studs. They provide a nailing surface for the exterior sheathing panels and the interior wallboard installed later. Small horizontal members sometimes nailed between the studs, called blocking, serve to align the studs to plumb and provide extra nailing surfaces.

Wall construction (each level)
Approx. time (days):....1-2
Cum. time (days):....25-36

Lingo:

plate material—a horizontally set piece of wood used flat, or on its wider edge or face, at either the bottom or the top of vertical members, as in a framed wall section.

cripple studs—vertical members under the bottom plate (or horizontal piece) of a window opening; also used to hold up either end of a header across the top of a door or window opening.

Once the floor joists and other framing members are in place, sheathing panels add stability to the platform and create a work surface for the rest of the framing stages.   Photo: Trus Joist MacMillan

Despite modern materials and fastening techniques, home building is in many ways the same as it was a century ago.

Photo: Trus Joist MacMillan

On raised-floor platforms, the walls are often constructed flat, then raised up along the perimeter and nailed and braced to be plumb and level. On concrete slab platforms, the framer may unbolt the sill plate and build the walls as if on a wood platform, or simply build vertically with the sill plate bolted in place—toe-nailing (or angling) the nails from the studs into the sill plate to secure them. The number and size of nails used is regulated by the building code, though many framers simply rely on their experience and tradition more so than a code book.

The most common wall-framing material is the 2x4. Its dimension actually measures 1.75 inches by 3.5 inches out of the lumber mill. The distance between the vertical studs is 16 inches from the center of each stud, called "on-center" spacing. The resulting 3.5-inch-deep cavity between the studs accommodates insulation, wiring, plumbing and various other materials.

When more insulation is required or specified for exterior walls, the builder may use larger, 2x6 members for the sills and walls, resulting in a 5.5-inch-deep cavity. In addition, the thicker exterior walls add bulk to the structure and, aesthetically, allow deeper window

Lingo:

plumb—exact vertical, typically determined by a plumb bob (a cone-shaped metal weight on the end of a long string).

toe-nailing—inserting a nail or other fastener at an angle.

Photo: Trus Joist MacMillan

Pneumatic tools, such as this nailer, have replaced hand or manual tools in the field.

sills and other features. Also, with the extra structural ability of 2x6 walls, the framer may space them 24 inches on center to save materials without sacrificing performance.

Whether 2x4 or 2x6, all wall-framing components are kept to the same dimension so that they align, or are "flush," with each other, creating a flat nailing surface for sheathing and drywall. However, while the exterior walls may be 2x6, the uninsulated and non-load-bearing interior walls are almost always constructed of 2x4s.

On a raised-floor platform, the exterior walls are nailed from the sill plate to the floor joists. For this reason, framers are careful to avoid

Lingo:

on-center spacing—the distance between structural members, such as wall studs, floor joists and roof trusses.

framing cavity—the space, including the depth, between structural members, typically wall studs.

load-bearing—a piece or section that supports weight from above.

51

A complete house frame, indicating the basic form of the finished home.

Photo: Trus Joist MacMillan

aligning the vertical studs directly over the joists, thus allowing the bottom plate to be nailed into the joists below.

The bottom plates for interior walls that are built parallel to the floor joists are typically aligned directly over the floor framing

TAKE NOTE: Straps and hold-downs

TAKE NOTE

To combat seismic and high-wind hazards, some building codes require additional support to connect the frame to the foundation. Long, thin metal straps, pre-drilled with nailing holes, are embedded in the slab or foundation walls at key points. Once the exterior walls go up, the straps are nailed to the studs. In more extreme cases, the builder or foundation contractor may also be required to install hold-downs—heavy-gauge metal connectors that increase the strength of the anchor-bolt connection. Occasionally, hold-downs extend all the way to the second-floor platform.

The point of this extra rigidity is to create a continuous load path from the top of the house down to the foundation and footings—a monolithic structure that can better resist structural damage from earthquakes and high winds. By design, a load placed or forced upon the house is transferred throughout the structure to accommodate the stress and relieve a single point or section of the house from bearing the entire brunt—and potentially failing as a result.

members below. Those aligned perpendicular to the joists are secured similarly to the exterior walls. Load-bearing interior walls are almost always set perpendicular to the joists and may require doubling the joists below them to accommodate the extra weight they carry.

On a slab foundation, the bolted sill plates along the perimeter secure the exterior walls. Interior walls are fastened to the concrete with long nails shot through the sill with a gun.

Regardless of the foundation, the framed walls are braced on both sides until they can be supported laterally, especially at the corners. While the framed walls at each corner are often nailed together at that connection, their true lateral strength comes from sheathing panels applied to the outside wall. That's why, on certain days during framing, you'll see only the corners of the house sheathed in plywood or another type of panel, with the rest of the walls left open, so that those critical areas are adequately supported.

Plated roof trusses have become a standard in residential roof framing.

Photo: Jason Munroe/Idaho Truss

Photo: Jason Munroe/Idaho Truss

The uniformity of plated trusses on simple roof designs makes them a cost-efficient and time-saving choice among builders, replacing on-site roof framing.

Lingo:

vaulted ceilings—angled or pitched ceilings, as opposed to flat.

roof pitches—the slope of the roof, from peak or ridge to the eaves.

Roof construction (plated trusses)

Approx. time (days): 1
Cum. time (days):....26-37

Once all of the exterior walls are constructed on the first-floor plat-form, either another platform is constructed for the second-floor liv-ing space, or the roof trusses are built and installed.

In the case of a two-story house, the same steps apply as to the first platform frame: the top plate of the walls serve as the bottom plate for the second-floor joists. As on the first floor, a supporting beam may also be necessary. The beams and joists are often held in place with joist hangers, metal seats that are nailed to the plate or beam and to both sides of each joist. A plywood subfloor completes the next platform, with the second-floor walls built up from there.

Roof Framing

If the house has only one above-grade living area (a single-story house), the exterior walls and often a few interior walls, support the weight of the roof. For most subdivision homes, the roof is con-structed with factory-built, or plated, trusses—so called because of the metal plates that connect the 2-by members of the truss.

Plated trusses are fabricated at a local factory or lumberyard and delivered to the job site, stacked and bound, by a flatbed truck. For simple roof designs, where the slope and span are repeated across the structure, pre-built plated trusses save significant time and money. Increasingly, plated trusses are fabricated in several shapes

54

and styles to accommodate vaulted ceilings or varied roof pitches and angles while still offering cost and time savings.

Most often, the trusses are hoisted into place by a small crane supplied either by the truss supplier or the framing contractor. Depending on the size and complexity of the roof design, the entire structure can be installed in a day or less using plated trusses.

For more complicated roofs, where the efficiency of plated trusses no longer applies, builders and framers revert to stick-framing the roof structure. More costly in terms of materials and labor, stick-framing a roof can occupy a week or two of a framing crew's time.

Roof framing by hand is one of the most complicated skills in home building. It requires the most accuracy, precise cuts and connections (often at difficult and compound angles) and consideration for additional measures to combat snow, wind, attic ventilation and other factors that put stress on the roof.

For instance, each rafter (the diagonal or sloping member) must be cut with an angled slot—called a bird's mouth—to make a solid connection at the wall's top plate. That connection is often held by nails as well as an angled, metal bracket on each side of the rafter. At the ridge—the top-most beam that carries or supports the weight of the rafters—the framers have to make the precise angle cuts on every rafter to maintain a flat, consistent slope (or pitch).

Often, roof framing must accommodate features like dormers, skylights, chimneys, vent pipes and other intrusions, as well as a consistent length to create the eaves or overhang detail. If the attic space is to be lived in, the rafters and ridge beam must be at a high enough pitch with adequate lateral support. Meanwhile, the bottom chords (the horizontal members that create the ceiling for the space below) must be strong enough to act as floor joists, as well, for the livable attic space above.

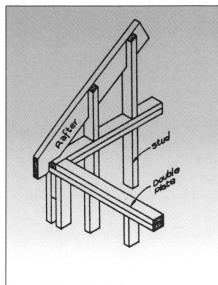

From: *Dwelling House Construction*

Roof construction (stick framing)
Approx. time (days): 5
Cum. time (days):....30-42

A typical roof rafter frame detail for a gable-end.

Lingo:

eaves—The bottom edges or other portions of the roof that extend beyond the outside walls of the house.

rafters—a series of sloping, parallel structural framing members that form the shape of the roof.

stick-framing—industry term for platform framing, with "sticks" being the individual pieces of wood or steel used to assemble the structural frame.

bird's mouth—the cut (or cuts) made at the end of a roof rafter or roof truss that allows it to rest on top of the intersecting wall.

pitch—the angle or slope of the roof.

55

Photo: Simpson Strong-Tie Company

Shear walls are separate or specially built wall panels that add stability for homes in high wind or earthquake-prone areas.

Sheathing

The final stage of rough framing is the sheathing. Already, the corners of the building may have been sheathed to provide lateral support for the exterior walls. Now, the rest of the frame (walls and roof) is covered on the outside by plywood or OSB panels, the same material used for the platform of each raised or framed floor.

TAKE NOTE

Lingo:

equilibrium moisture content—the point at which the moisture content of wood or lumber is equal to the relative humidity (or moisture content) of its environment.

warp—a distortion of shape from wood shrinkage along one edge or plane.

> ### TAKE NOTE: Shear walls
>
> Additional sheathing might be applied to one or more interior walls or even on concrete foundation walls below grade, which indicates shear-wall construction. Shear walls are built as extra protection against extreme lateral stresses and forces, such as earthquakes or hurricanes. Many local building departments, such as those in South Florida and California, require shear walls in every new home constructed in their jurisdiction.
>
> In some areas of the country, in fact, the shear walls may be the only place where a builder might use solid panels of sheathing. On the main exterior frame, let-in bracing—long strips of metal or 2x4s notched and nailed into a framed wall section at a diagonal—provides adequate lateral support, with panels of thin rigid foam serving to enclose the framing envelope and deliver insulating value beyond wood sheathing panels.

Depending on the builder or framer's style of sheathing a house, solid panels (either foam or wood) are often installed and nailed to the studs and other framing members without regard to window and door openings ... yet. Rather than measuring an opening and trying to make an accurate cut-out for a window or door on the ground before installation, many framers will nail the panels to the walls and roof and then come back and cut out the openings to ensure accuracy.

As with the structural frame components, building codes dictate the size, type and pattern of nails to properly secure sheathing panels to the frame. These specifications are examined by the building official as part of the rough-frame inspection upon completion of this phase. Some common problems: Roof sheathing nails that miss their intended targets (the structural rafters), not enough nails in

Lingo:

twist—a distortion of shape from wood shrinkage along two edges or planes.

check—a split running parallel to the grain of the wood or lumber, caused by shrinkage.

lumber load—the lumber delivery to the job site.

nail pops—the showing of nail heads in a finished wall, caused by shrinkage of the wood framing.

When Wood Shrinks

As framing lumber evolves from a tree to a 2x4, it begins to lose the moisture accumulated in its fibers. Either passively (by air), or mechanically in a kiln, drying to a moisture content of about 19 percent helps ensure the lumber will maintain its shape in the lumberyard, on the job site and during framing. Drying lumber to between 11 and 20 percent moisture content helps balance the weight, workability and shrinkage potential of the wood.

In fact, it is preferable to allow framing lumber to adjust to a particular climate before it is installed. Doing so allows the lumber to reach what's called an equilibrium moisture content that is compatible with the relative humidity of its surrounding environment.

If lumber is allowed or forced to dry to the point that its cells begin to lose moisture, the wood begins to shrink. For instance, lumber cut in the timber baskets of the Pacific Northwest and shipped to dry, hot Las Vegas has been known to twist and warp beyond use within hours of being delivered to the lumberyard or job site—the climate shock was just too dramatic.

It doesn't help that more of today's lumber is harvested from younger and smaller trees. Such timber, grown on private land or tree farms, lacks the structural maturity and fiber strength to accommodate the natural drying process as cut lumber.

Depending on the cut of the lumber, shrinkage can occur in the form of warp, twist, bend or check. The latter manifests as cracks along the surface of the lumber. Of all these problems, checking is the least troublesome. In fact, in larger timbers (6-bys and larger), checking is anticipated by groups who calculate and publish span and load charts. (Knots in wood are similarly accounted for in span and load tables.)

Lumber that shrinks is usable, but not preferred. Particularly bent or twisted pieces may be cut for blocking or cripple studs. Occasionally, the lumber load (or a portion of it) is rejected by the builder or framer and returned to the lumberyard, often delaying construction as a result.

In a completed house, lumber that continues to shrink, or perhaps shrink and swell due to seasonal climate changes, can cause a multitude of problems. Floor squeaks, sticky windows and nail pops are common symptoms. Because milled lumber is of increasingly poor quality, builders and framers are looking to alternatives to avoid or mitigate these and other problems.

metal connectors like joist hangers and hurricane straps and using a too-small framing member for a given structural load. Most of these problems can be addressed on the spot. If not, they must be fixed before the next stage—installation of the rough mechanicals—can start.

Why Wood?

The history of American home building centers on the use of wood as its prevailing structural material. Besides Canada, with its vast raw timber supplies, the U.S. is the only country in the world that relies primarily, almost exclusively, on wood for home construction. The rest of the world uses concrete and other earth-borne materials (such as adobe), or, as in Japan, imported timber from North America that is milled for their factory-built housing industries.

Wood is so ingrained in our building culture that it drives building codes, framing practices, engineering design and the approvals and inspection process, not to mention the world commodities market. Any hitch or use of alternative methods or material is a shock to the system. Only a few efficiencies, such as plated trusses, plywood and wood I-joists, are now considered standard and accepted practice.

In recent years, however, the well-heeled timber industry has been at odds with environmental concerns regarding timber harvesting and the conservation of public forests. The debate has led to restrictions on traditional timber resources milled into lumber and other materials, the increased use of younger and non-traditional trees and a general reduction in the quality and reliability of today's milled framing lumber.

Lingo:

industrialized housing—factory-built or pre-manufactured housing that is either delivered to or assembled on a job site. Also, modular, manufactured or HUD-code housing.

modular homes—homes in which the majority of construction occurs in a factory setting.

panelized wall sections—sections of framed walls built in a factory and delivered to the job site.

For the housing industry, the most dramatic impact so far came in the mid-1990s. In just a few month's time, the price of lumber nearly doubled from a decade earlier. Timber companies and lumberyards, sensing further price spikes, were hesitant to extend price guarantees to builders and framing contractors, disrupting the delicate balance between the cost to build a house and a marketable price to sell it. And, despite the extra cost (whether incurred by the builder or passed to the home buyer), the quality of the lumber was still poor.

Alternatives to Wood Framing

The lumber price spikes of 1994-95 also resulted in use of alternative structural materials for housing, many of which had been lingering in the shadows of the industry for decades.

Photo: Structural Insulated Panel Assn.

Structural insulated panels (or SIPs) are a time-saving method for wall framing.

One technology those that made significant inroads was industrialized housing that involved structural components made in factories instead of fabricated on the job site. Factories that produced modular homes, panelized wall sections and pre-built components (such as plated trusses) could better absorb lumber price fluctuations because they bought in such large quantities. They also offered factory quality control and faster on-site assembly by an ever-shrinking skilled labor force.

Like factory-built framing, engineered wood products gained popularity among builders. Large-dimension joists, beams and other components are made of reconstituted wood fibers. In addition, the timber source of this fiber is increasingly from smaller and non-traditional timber sources that are not included in the environmental fray.

In comparable dimension, engineered wood is more reliable and of better quality than even the best-quality solid wood. Thus, wood I-joists replaced 2x10s; glued veneer lumber beams replaced solid, 4-by headers and other large timbers.

Lingo:

pre-built components—sections of a house frame or structure built in a factory and delivered to the job site, such as plated roof trusses and panelized wall sections.

glued veneer lumber—pieces of milled lumber glued together through heat and pressure to create a larger beam; also called a glulam beam.

And because these products were derived from the same source as those they replaced (wood), builders and framers were more comfortable with them than some of the non-wood alternatives to lumber. Environmentalists also applauded the more efficient use of timber to make them and, in addition, the superior strength of engineered lumber reduced the amount of wood required to build a house. Today, nearly half of all new homes are built with engineered lumber in some structural capacity.

Light-gauge steel framing also made headlines during the mid-'90s. Historically reserved for multi-story buildings and commercial/industrial construction, steel components offered a higher level of quality—studs that didn't warp and lightweight members of significantly more strength. Steel also offered a well-established industry looking for a new market.

But, unlike engineered lumber, steel was a different material requiring new skills and tools. Builders found it difficult to hire steel framers and get a reliable stream of material from a local supplier. Now, light-gauge steel is used sparingly in home construction, mostly for interior, non-loadbearing walls where standard 2x4s are of such poor quality as to push the use of steel. The all-steel house, at least on a production scale, is still in the wings.

Lingo:

light-gauge steel—steel components made from rolled steel as opposed to welded, heavy-gauge steel.

A newer method for above-grade wall construction is the use of insulated concrete forms (or ICFs), which replace wood-framed walls with concrete.

Photo: Insulated Concrete Form Assn.

Photo: North American Steel Framing Alliance

Steel-framed homes are gaining acceptance as alternatives to wood-frame construction.

Of the other alternatives to traditional lumber framing, structural insulated panels (SIPs) offer some advantages. Factory-built, these 4x8-foot (and larger) panels feature a layer of solid foam insulation laminated between sections of plywood—essentially, complete and insulated structural wall and roof sections. While not yet in the mainstream of housing production, SIPs have gained a foothold in cold-climate markets and as a substrate in post-and-beam or timber-frame-built homes.

Post-and-beam (P&B) construction, unlike construction with SIPs or engineered wood, was a popular home-building method in the U.S. during the 18th and 19th centuries, and was later replaced by more efficient practices using smaller and lighter dimension lumber. Imagine a old-fashioned barn raising and that's post-and-beam: large timbers spaced far apart, connected by mortise-and-tenon joints and wood pegs forming the basic structure of a house or other building.

Today, traditionalists still build post-and-beam homes the same way, while a cottage industry of more industrialized components and methods also has emerged. SIPs are often used between the large framing timbers of a P&B house because of their insulating value and bulk.

Lingo:

substrate—a backing for another surface to be applied later.

mortise-and-tenon joints—a connection between two pieces, typically wood, where a recessed cut in one piece (the mortise) receives a projecting cut from the other (the tenon), securing the pieces together.

61

Despite timber restrictions and higher costs for lumber, wood is by far the predominant framing materials for new housing.

Photo: Rich Binsacca

As is P&B construction, masonry and concrete are centuries-old ways of building shelter. Because of the vast timber resources of North America, however, neither became more than secondary structural materials for mass-produced housing. Most commonly, concrete blocks and poured concrete are used for foundations and other below- or at-grade conditions (see Chapter 2), as well as flat-work (driveways, patios) and in decorative applications, such as pavers. In most parts of the country, only brick and stucco have a significant presence above grade as exterior finish materials over wood-framed homes. However, in some parts of Florida and other hurricane areas, concrete block is mandated by code or preferred by homeowners and builders for the above-grade wall structure.

One concrete material, however, is making moves to gain a larger share of the housing construction pie: insulated concrete forms, or ICFs (covered more extensively in Chapter 2, page 32). Though far from the current mainstream practices, ICFs offer the well-established structural advantages of concrete in an easy-to-use form. The ICF industry also has done well to incorporate wood and steel framing into its specifications and guidelines, where appropriate, to ease anxiety among builders. Like steel, however, it currently suffers from a lack of skilled labor and a steady source of locally available material (the forms, not the concrete).

Lingo:

stucco—a cement plaster applied to the exterior wall or surface of a building as a finish.

Finally, a few creative types have tapped into regional and historical methods, including rammed earth, adobe and straw-bale construction, in reaction to the changes occurring in the traditional milled lumber industry. These methods, while structurally sound when properly engineered, are too labor intensive to ever replace stick-built construction. ■

Lingo:

rammed earth—a building process by which a mixture of dirt, aggregate and water is hard-pressed into forms to create structural walls.

adobe—A clay substance used to make unfired brick, which can then be stacked and mortared to create walls or other structural components.

straw-bale—A building process by which bound bales of straw (dried hay) are stacked and reinforced to create structural, load-bearing walls and other components.

Rough Mechanicals

Photo: HGTV

As the framing stage nears completion, the installation of plumbing, heating and electrical systems begins.

Once the home's structural frame is done, perhaps even before the exterior sheathing is completely applied, a steady stream of specialty contractors invade the job site to install what are called rough, mechanicals. The installation of plumbing, electrical and heating and cooling systems is a two-step process for each. The first, or "rough," stage is the behind-the-wall interworkings of these and other distribution and disposal systems, while a finish stage for each occurs later.

The three main mechanical systems of a home are electrical, plumbing (including natural gas, if appropriate) and heating, ventilation and air conditioning (commonly referred to as HVAC). Each requires its own crew of workers to install.

Lingo:

mechanicals—a broad term referring to the plumbing, electrical, heating and cooling and other utility-driven operating systems in the house; specifically, may be used as synonym for the HVAC systems only.

65

Additional services, such as cable television, in-home security, telephone and data wiring and fire sprinkler systems are also installed at this time. Usually, only a few additional contractors are required for these secondary networks, as systems like security and telephone/data are often handled by the same subcontractor.

There is no prescribed order as to which rough system is installed first, though savvy builders will often gather the various subcontractors early on (sometimes prior to excavation) to discuss their respective schedules and decide the order. At that meeting, the specialty contractors also may identify framing details—like a beam or header—that might intrude on their work. Or, they may suggest changes to the framing plan that would make their jobs easier and faster without sacrificing structural integrity or the overall design of the house.

Before Installation

It is the builder's responsibility to make sure two things are ready before he or she calls the mechanical subs to start their rough installations: the frame is completed and the various services are brought into the house by their respective utilities. During construction, the utilities are typically kept in the builder's name (or company name) until close of escrow, at which time the homeowners assume responsibility for the accounts.

TAKE NOTE: Framing alterations

Once the mechanical subs arrive, you'll start to see the frame of the house change a bit, namely as it gets cut up to accommodate the various wires, pipes and other conduits. Notches, holes and other cuts are precisely calculated—and inspected by the building department—to avoid any impact on the home's structural integrity. Some framing materials, in fact, are manufactured to accommodate electrical wiring and other systems. Engineered I-joists, for instance, feature small, pre-stamped (or perforated) holes along the center of the joist, which can be punched out for wires and pipes.

Lingo:

close of escrow—settlement of the deed; when title and deed to the house and property are transferred from the seller (the builder) to the buyer or homeowner after certain legal and financial conditions are met.

notches—sections cut out to accommodate another piece so that it is flush to the surface or relies on the first section for support.

Scheduling

In some cases, especially in larger homes, mechanical contractors may be scheduled to work at the same time, though not in the same area. Often, however, they work almost like a relay team, passing each other at the site trailer.

Allowing a sub to work autonomously has its advantages, mostly because the complete installation of one system's rough is a guideline to the installation and placement of the others. Whatever time efficiencies might be gained by having two or more subs at the house at a time are often washed away when a plumbing stub-up intrudes on a wiring run.

Inspections

In addition, each rough-mechanical installation is required to be inspected by the building department upon its completion, often before the next sub can come in and certainly before any rough systems are covered up.

Occasionally, some specialty contractors will perform similar tasks. For instance, the electrician may need to install a rigid metal conduit, similar to a plumbing pipe, to house his wires; the HVAC contractor is required to run low-voltage wiring from the heating and cooling equipment to connect the thermostats and other controls. Even so, most electricians would be lost if asked to sweat pipes or run a gas line.

Service Drop

Most utilities enter the house at the same point, or at least into the same area, whether it be the basement, crawlspace, attic, garage or utility room. The "service drop" is the first point of attachment from the utility to the house and is the starting point for each specialty contractor's run of wires, pipes, conduits or ductwork. Ideally, this area is centrally located in the house and easily accessed by the contractors and the homeowners.

If possible, the builder and homeowner should agree on the location of the service drop to avoid any unsightly meters or utility conduits along an exterior elevation. If the utilities are already dropped before the homeowner is on board, the builder may work to disguise the meter or point of entry or run an extra length of conduit to shift its location away from view.

The installation of rough-mechanicals results in a maze of pipes, wires and metal ducts (or conduits for the HVAC), all of which is brought to a point ready to finish. Electrical wires are connected to a receptacle or switch, ready for a faceplate; pipes stick out of the wall or floor, capped and waiting for an appliance or plumbing fixture; the duct openings extend into the floors and ceilings of each room, awaiting louvered registers.

The rough mechanicals remain in their unfinished state until the drywall and most of the other interior finishes are applied, at which

Lingo:

gas line—the pipe that delivers natural gas or propane to an appliance.

conduit—a hollow gateway, typically a length of pipe that carries and protects wires, water or other utility.

faceplate—a plastic or metal plate that fits over an electrical outlet or switch to protect and cover the wiring.

fixture—a product fixed to the structure, most commonly regarding plumbing products such as toilets, tubs and sinks, or lighting, such as in a ceiling.

duct—the conduit through which forced air (heated, cooled or exhausted), is delivered.

Photo: Rich Binsacca

With engineered wood I-joists, wiring can be run through pre-stamped knock-out holes in the webs, eliminating the need for separately framed chases or conduits.

time the builder or site superintendent recalls the subcontractors to complete their work. The "finish" stage is covered in Chapter 7.

Electrical

There are two primary types of wiring in a house: high voltage and low voltage. Electrical contractors almost exclusively install the high-voltage systems that provide electricity for lighting and appli-

Photo: Trus Joist MacMillan

Wiring is typically the only mechanical system run through exterior walls.

ances. Low-voltage systems, which serve security, entertainment, communications, environmental control and other functions, are usually installed by another specialty contractor.

High- and low-voltage wiring systems operate from separate central (or service) panels, the hubs at the service drop that contain the connection from the utilities and control the distribution of electricity in the house. High-voltage service is first run through a meter mounted on the outside of the house before entering the structure and the service box inside; low-voltage systems rarely, if ever, involve a meter. Most of these systems are serviced by cable and phone or data lines, allowing remote monitoring by the provider.

Electrical rough
Approx. time (days): 2
Cum. time (days):....28-39

The National Electrical Code (NEC) and the design of the high-voltage service panel dictate which wires control what areas of the house, as well as specific appliances that require dedicated power, like the washer and dryer, furnace and water heater.

For all high-voltage electrical wiring, the NEC dictates the amp (or ampere, the amount of the electrical current at the circuit) and the

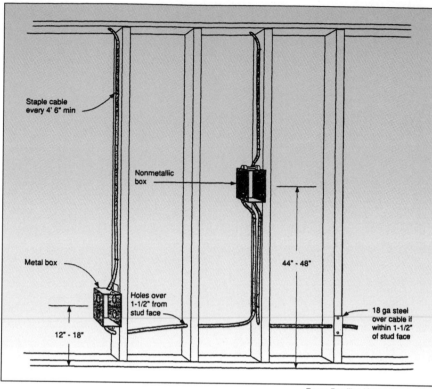

Staple cable
every 4' 6" min

Nonmetallic
box

Metal box

44" - 48"

Holes over
1-1/2" from
stud face

18 ga steel
over cable if
within 1-1/2"
of stud face

12" - 18"

The elements of a common electrical rough installation, showing both vertical and horizontal runs within the wall cavity.

From: *Dwelling House Construction*

voltage (the actual power delivered from one point to another) for a given demand.

For general lighting and electrical services, a 15-amp circuit and 110-volt wire can service about 600 square feet of space or about a dozen receptacles (switches, outlets and ceiling fixtures). Large appliances are required to be serviced by a dedicated circuit of at least 20 amps and a single run of wire up to 240 volts to provide adequate electrical power for their separate operation.

Daisy Chain

For high-voltage wiring, the prevailing design for providing electricity to a room or area of the house is called a daisy chain. Simply, a single, high-voltage wire (either 110 or 220, depending on what electrical demand it will incur), powered by a circuit at the central panel, brings power to a variety of receptacles in a given room.

Lingo:

tripped circuit—the automatic disabling of an electrical circuit when it is overloaded or dysfunctional.

The wire's connection at a receptacle not only delivers electricity to that spot on the wall or ceiling, but links to another wire that carries the same signal to the next receptacle, and so on. The resulting

Photo: Kevin Berne

Today's complicated and sophisticated wiring schemes often require more than one electrical control panel in the house.

"chain" ends, or terminates, at the last receptacle the wire and circuit are designed to service. All receptacles along the chain are "hard wired," which simply means that electricity is constantly flowing to them, waiting for someone to plug in an appliance or flip a switch.

Not only does a typical daisy chain service several receptacles at a time, a "tripped" or disabled circuit resulting from overloaded

Wires are fed through their respective outlets and allowed to dangle until the electrician comes back to finish the job.

Photo: Dow Chemical

Lingo:

speculative housing— homes that are designed and built on the prospect of being sold during construction or upon completion.

allowances (code and budget)— in the building code, the acceptance of similar, if not exact, provisions that meet the code; in budget terms, an amount of money provided to the buyer for the purchase of certain items or products of their choice, such as appliances and light fixtures.

walk-through— a buyer's tour and inspection of the house, typically occurring upon the completion of the home.

bits— blades for a drill or drill motor.

demand affects only that chain, not the whole house. Modern circuit breakers, unlike fuses that literally burned out when overloaded, simply need to be switched back on after the offending appliances (lamps, televisions, VCRs) are unplugged and connected elsewhere. Rarely is the wiring behind the wall damaged.

Codes

Codes not only dictate amps and voltage, but some minimum standards to enhance the safety and security of the homeowners. For instance, the NEC requires hard-wired lighting fixtures (as opposed to plug-in lamps) in the kitchen, baths, and entry. Similarly, a hard-wired switch must control light fixtures (including lamps) in halls, stairways, attached garages and all habitable spaces.

Placement

What codes don't dictate is the precise placement of receptacles (except beyond a certain height or distance from water sources, such as the kitchen sink) or the number of receptacles along a length of wall. In speculative housing construction, the builder and electrician decide where to place the outlets and switches. Typically, this decision is based on experience and feel: switches are placed on the edges of a wall or just inside a door; outlets are centered on a short wall or evenly spaced on a longer section. Usually, the placement is adequate for a typical homeowner's needs.

Closed-loop Systems

So-called "smart home" wiring schemes have been introduced in recent years to combat the inherent dangers of traditional, high-voltage house wiring. Some of these systems work on a closed-loop design where each receptacle has a dedicated wire that originates from and terminates back at the service box or electrical panel.

Such schemes also are designed to deliver electricity only when it is demanded (such as a switch being turned on, or the operation of a small appliance). Just plugging in a given fixture won't activate the circuit. And, the computer-controlled hub recognizes overloads before they happen, denying electricity to an offending appliance or fixture.

Closed-loop systems are rare in high-voltage house wiring, if only because they buck traditional methods, require new tools and materials and necessitate that the appliances themselves contain complex microchips that "talk" to the computer-controlled panel, a feature few (if any) of today's lamps and toasters contain.

Still, the closed-loop concept has found a foothold in low-voltage schemes. Home run or star-wired systems mimic the dedicated wires and closed-loop design for telephone, data, security, communications and environmental control features that are becoming increasingly popular in today's new homes.

The benefits of a star-wired, low-voltage telephone and data wiring scheme are different than for high-voltage wiring. Shock is not the major concern; rather, the ability to offer high-speed access to voice, data, fax and other lines—and a dedicated outside line for each—is the true advantage of star-wiring. Imagine never having to worry about tying up the phone while you surf the Internet, or easily adding a new phone line to accommodate an additional computer or other high-tech gizmo.

But if you're able to be involved in the decision-making process, helping determine the placement of the electrical receptacles in your new home will pay off in added convenience. Most builders are open to your input. After all, it's an easy thing to adjust before the electrician arrives, and the sub could care less (within code allowances) exactly where to "spot" each receptacle.

If you're given the opportunity, try to imagine what furniture and functions you'll have along each wall in the house, as well as any physical limitations that might hinder your ability to reach a switch or outlet. While the decision may have to be done on the building plans, you may have time during the framing stage to walk through the house and get a better perspective on where you want outlets, switches and overhead lighting receptacles. In fact, many builders schedule a "walk-through" of the framed house before the mechan-

> **TAKE NOTE: Conduits**
> Occasionally, you may see a rigid metal pipe, or conduit, fastened to the wall frame to carry bundles of wires. Conduits are used on particularly long runs or when there are several wires going to one location or area of the house. Without a conduit, large bundles are more difficult to properly secure to the wall frame, creating sags or pinches that can affect electrical performance. The rigid metal also protects the wires, eliminating protective faceplates.

ical subs arrive to explain the building process, update the job's progress and make any minor adjustments.

Wiring vs. Framing

Electrical wiring, whether high or low voltage, almost always runs through and around the structural frame. An electrician's crew is outfitted with power drills and bits that cut through the center of each stud, creating a series of holes through which the wires are pulled and chained together; vertical runs are attached snug to the sides of the studs with insulated brackets. For a typical house, the electrical rough is about a two-day job; upon completion, this stage is inspected by the building department for adherence to the NEC and other local requirements.

To protect wires from intruding nails or other fasteners, electrical runs within a framed wall are required to be at least 1½ inches away from the face of the studs or other framing member. That, or they must be guarded by small, steel faceplates set into the stud. Some electricians do both for added protection and to more easily pass inspection.

Lingo:

grounding—the direct or indirect conduction of electricity to the ground or earth.

GFI/ground fault interrupter—a device that ensures grounding of the wire to protect against electrical shock or short circuits.

> **TAKE NOTE: Finding a stud**
> If you want to find a wall stud to secure a picture hanger or nail, look for the outlets along the wall. These receptacles are nailed to the sides of the wall studs, typically on the right side because most electricians (like most people) are right-handed. From the nearest corner, measure just to the left of the outlet's faceplate and you should find a stud (if not, try the other side of the outlet), then transfer that measurement from the same corner to the height of your nail. To find another stud on the same wall, measure 16 inches either way from any known stud location—the typical spacing between studs in residential construction.
> If the house is framed with steel, the process requires only that you drag a magnet along the finished wall. If it sticks to the wall, you've found a stud.

However, because most horizontal wiring runs are located along the lower section of the wall (for the placement of outlets), and are attached to the sides of the vertical studs and ceiling joists for switches and fixtures higher up on the wall, there's little chance of hitting a wire with a picture hanger or even a drywall nail.

For most of us, electricity is something we take for granted, and therefore know little about. For that reason, it's also a scary prospect when it breaks down, or even when we're faced with simply switching on a tripped circuit. That gray metal box is intimidating, mostly because we're clueless about what it contains.

The NEC, for one, takes our fear into account, while at the same time protecting the system from overloads and damage. In new homes, the code requires the grounding of the electrical service at the panel, eliminating the chance of a person getting shocked if they touch the box, use a tool to repair damage or plug in an appliance. In addition, the use (and requirement) of a ground-fault interrupter (or GFI) futher protects us from high-voltage electrical shocks.

Such provisions, however, don't relieve you of proper respect for electricity. Exposed wires carry an electrical current; touch them the wrong way, and you become a conduit for that current (read: a shock). Similarly, damaged or frayed wires, when sparked by a connection, cause hundreds of house fires a year. Constant overloading of a circuit may eventually damage the system, creating an unseen fire hazard and requiring extensive repair.

Plumbing
Distribution
Like electrical wiring, plumbing is a basic distribution system. It delivers water and natural gas through a network of varying-sized pipes. But plumbing also concerns issues of waste disposal, both solid and gaseous, that require another set of pipes and vents through the structural frame and out to sewer services and the outside air.

Plumbing rough
Approx. time (days): 3
Cum. time (days):....31-42

Because plumbing pipes, for distribution and disposal, are larger and more intrusive than electrical wiring, the house frame is typically designed and built to accommodate the system with minimum adjustment by the plumbing contractor. Tight vertical and horizontal areas, called chases, are designed into the framing plan to hide and protect pipes from the finished living spaces (chases also serve to house ductwork for the HVAC system).

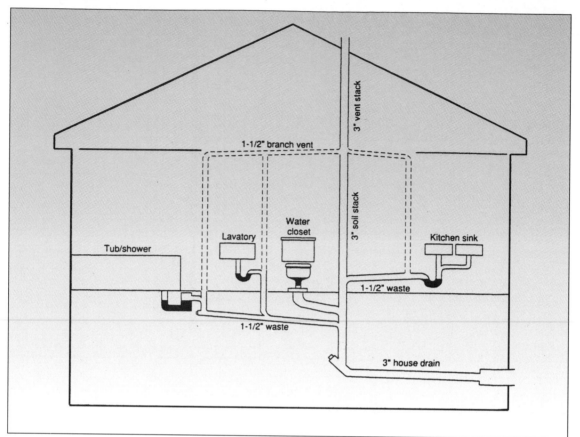

The elements of a common drain-waste-vent (DWV) plumbing design for a residential setting.

From: *Dwelling House Construction*

Lingo:

spotting a fixture—marking the location of or installing a product that is fixed to the structure.

freeze-thaw cycles—the systematic freezing and thawing of elements or products, such as plumbing pipes, which mat result in damage or failure.

combustion appliance—natural gas-operated appliances or equipment that rely on combustion air to fuel (or allow to burn) the natural gas.

In addition, the floor plan of the house is designed, in part, with the plumbing system in mind. While tradition, convenience, the family's needs and traffic flow all help determine the arrangement of rooms in a house, so does the location of the various plumbing fixtures in relation to each other.

Often, to save the plumber's time, accommodate the framing layout and limit the extent of the plumbing runs from the service drop, the floor plan will show "plumbing walls." That is, water-using rooms are placed adjacent to one another, as with the kitchen and laundry area, where the pipes servicing appliances for both are located on the same length of wall. Back-to-back situations, such as placing (or spotting) the bathroom's lavatory, toilet and tub-shower fixtures on the other side of the same wall of the kitchen sink or gas range, accomplish the same goal.

To guard against freeze-thaw cycles, plumbing pipes are generally kept out of exterior walls. Again, like plumbing walls, this practice is a subtle consideration with a practical reason. Rarely, if ever, do such decisions and designs affect the convenience or aesthetic value of a home. Occasionally, codes even prohibit plumbing pipes from being installed on outside walls in an effort to mitigate potential damage and failure from frozen pipes.

Natural Gas

Besides the distribution of water, plumbing also con-

Photo: Kevin Berne

Plumbing pipes, most often copper, weave throughout the structural frame, carrying either water or natural gas.

cerns delivery of natural gas for combustion appliances such as cooking ranges and ovens, clothes dryers, furnaces and heat pumps and water heaters. Because the pipes and other accessory products are similar in size and application to those for water and disposal, the plumbing contractor often installs gas lines, too. As with any service, natural gas is "dropped" or brought to the house or curb by the utility company for the contractor to connect to his or her work inside the house.

TAKE NOTE: Pipes

The most common plumbing pipe material is copper, but several others are approved by code for hot and cold water distribution. Rigid plastic (CPVC), galvanized steel and flexible plastic (polybutylene, or PB) all are approved for residential use, though local building departments may restrict or prohibit any or all in their jurisdictions. Each has its advantages and limitations; the key to any system's performance and reliability is its installation by a qualified plumbing contractor. So, too, are the terms of any product and system performance warranties by the builder, subcontractor, manufacturer or supplier.

Connecting Up

Specific to the water system, a variety of pipes are allowed by the National Plumbing Code (NPC) to carry both hot and cold water; others are limited to cold water only. The code also regulates the size and maximum length of pipes depending on their intended use and to facilitate the proper and balanced flow of water and waste.

Water arrives into the house from the street (or water main) cold. From the connection at the service drop inside the house, the plumber installs a branch pipe to the water heater, thereby supplying the house with hot water. The hot and cold lines then run in tandem to various appliances and fixtures that require both.

Standard plumbing pipes, regardless of the material used, start at the service drop at a ¾- to 1-inch dimension. As they connect to an appliance or fixture, the size is usually reduced by ¼-inch, which boosts the pressure and increases the flow of water at that point. By generating a steadier flow, smaller pipes also reduce potential imbalances in flow and temperature, even when another appliance or fixture is in use.

Because a home's network of plumbing pipes is always full of water, providing instant delivery at a given point, every stub-up has a shut-off valve. Like the valves that control a faucet's operation, the shut-off value opens and closes the flow of water.

Shut-off valves are an oval-like handle near where the pipe comes out of the wall. Should the faucet or toilet fail, for instance, the shut-off valve stops water from flowing to that fixture or appliance without requiring you to shut down the entire system.

TAKE NOTE: Water treatment systems

Increasingly, builders offer or install water treatment systems at the service drop. These so-called "point-of-entry" or POE systems balance the acidity of the water that flows throughout the house to guard against pipe corrosion and mineral build-up. Such systems may also address issues of color or odor common in treated municipal water supplies.

Often, though, such "aesthetic" qualities are addressed with point-of-use, or POU, water treatment products. Commonly located in a cabinet or vanity under the sink, POU systems filter incoming water before it reaches the tap. Recently, a few faucet manufacturers have introduced products with integral water filters, eliminating the sometimes cumbersome POU components.

Waste Disposal

The system for the disposal of waste and sewer gasses is termed "drain-waste-vent" or DWV. It includes varying-sized pipes and also relies on the design of certain fixtures that include a "trap," which seals off or blocks waste and gasses from reentering the living space. A toilet's trap, for instance, is contained in the curvature at the base of the fixture. The trap maintains a volume of water between the waste pipe and the bowl to block the passage of sewer gasses back into the bathroom.

While water delivery systems perform by pressure (allowing water to travel from the lower levels of a house to an upstairs bathroom), waste disposal works primarily by gravity. Waste and drain lines are either stacked (vertical) or branched (horizontal, with a slight downward slope). Stack pipes are usually large (four-inch) black cast iron or heavy-duty plastic, while branch pipes of the same material are narrower, perhaps just 1½-inches in diameter. Branch pipes from every water-using appliance and fixture (by code, all of them require a drain) eventually connect to a centrally located stack pipe, which then drains to a sewer or septic system.

Ventilation

By contrast, the ventilation of sewer gasses generated by waste water are exhausted up through the roof, where they dissipate in the open air. While both gas and solid waste use the same stack and branch pipes, they part ways at the stack or through smaller vertical pipes in the system that carry the gas up through the roof. Depending on the size of the house and the number of bathrooms, a roof may have up to a half-dozen hooded vents protruding from its slopes.

For an average-size house, installation of a complete plumbing rough-in takes about three days, at which time it is inspected by the building department.

HVAC

Of the three basic mechanical systems in a house, HVAC (heating, ventilating and air conditioning) is the most sophisticated. It involves complex equipment, a variety of energy sources and sensitive controls.

The HVAC system also may include ancillary products that filter and remove indoor air pollutants, regulate humidity levels, offer specific ventilation of moist or warm areas and capture and reuse heat from exhausted, conditioned air. And, more so than electricity and plumbing, the performance of the HVAC system is tied to the home's construction.

HVAC rough
Approx. time (days):....3-4
Cum. time (days):....34-36

Photo: Ideal Homes

Flexible ductwork, in this case contained in the attic space, is a lightweight alternative to solid, sheet metal ducts.

Lingo:

ductwork—the series of ducts leading to and from the furnace or other heating or cooling equipment throughout the house.

chase—a space or area in the structural frame provided for ductwork and other utility conduits to hide them from view.

Forced-air Systems

Most heating and cooling in today's homes is through forced-air systems. Depending on the season or climate, fans in the furnace or air conditioner blow air through a shared network of metal chases, called ducts, to rooms in the house. Louvered grills (registers) in the floor (or high up on the walls in some warm climates) can be opened or closed to regulate the flow of air, while the thermostat controls the temperature. Larger or centrally located rooms of the house also include a return register, usually in the ceiling, to exhaust stale air so that it can be refreshed with new air arriving from the furnace, air conditioner or other HVAC equipment.

For the most part, forced-air systems are either gas or electric, depending on the prevailing (or available) utilities for a given subdivision or neighborhood. The conditioned air itself contains no gas fumes or electric current. In fact, the utility simply powers the unit's network of heating coils, filters and blowers. Most new homes are built with a furnace for heat and an air conditioner for cool air; heat pumps combine the heating and cooling functions into one unit.

Capacity

The size, or capacity, of a given HVAC system depends on the size and design of the house, as well as the type of wall framing, insulation and other thermal measures, including windows and the home's orientation to the sun. Capacity is expressed in tonnage, while a unit's output (or ability to heat) is calculated in terms of Btus, or British thermal units.

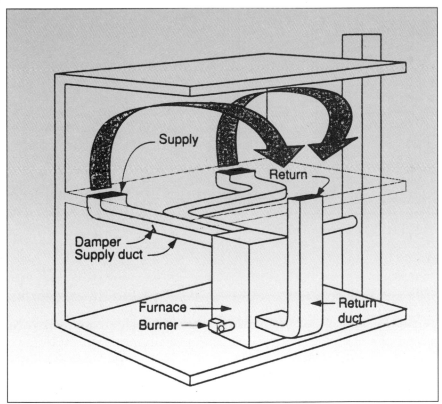

From: *How to Build a Wood-Framed House*

The dynamics of a typical forced-air heating and/or cooling system, where used or exhausted air is rerun through the system to conserve energy.

In larger homes (those over 3,000 square feet), or where home-owners want a dedicated system to a certain room or area, a second unit (or units) may be required. In that case, the functions of each unit are "zoned" to deliver conditioned air separately to specific areas of the house (such as upstairs or downstairs). Each unit has its own duct system, return air registers, thermostats and controls.

As a multi-unit scheme, zoned HVAC typically requires equipment of smaller capacity compared to a single unit servicing an entire house. The upside is that zoned systems offer better control of the indoor environment and, presumably as a result, energy efficiency.

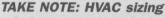

TAKE NOTE: HVAC sizing
An improperly sized HVAC unit or system—whether providing too much or too little capacity or Btus for the space it conditions—wastes energy and reduces the effective life of the equipment. An undersized furnace, for instance, must work harder and suck up more gas or electricity to heat the house, straining its interworkings in the process.

Ductwork

As with the other utilities servicing a house, it is best if the HVAC equipment is located in a central area of the house. Doing so reduces the amount of ductwork. Long "runs," or extensive lengths of ductwork, may not be able to sustain the temperature of the air traveling to a room at the other end of the house. Laying out and installing the ducts takes the bulk of an HVAC contractor's time on the job site. In all, installing a typical system takes about three or four days.

Long duct runs also have more potential for leaks, because there are more sections of ducts that can fail or become loose. Leaky ducts, in fact, are a primary cause of heat loss in homes, which affects the heating and cooling bills. And, longer runs are more fertile ground for molds and other indoor pollutants.

Duct material is typically made from thin sheet metal that is mould-ed and welded into rectangular or round, cylindrical sections. The sections are connected into "runs" by screws and duct tape (the intended use of that product), the latter sealing the joints between sections. Sheet metal is not only durable, but acts as a thermal con-ductor to help maintain temperature as the heated or cooled air travels through the ducts.

In some cases and especially in warmer regions of the country, duct runs are constructed of sections of coiled metal wrapped in a thin, insulated sheathing. A bright, reflective layer on the sheathing acts as a thermal barrier to block heated or cooled air from escaping.

The flexibility of these cylindrical ducts, while more difficult to connect and seal than sheet metal, makes them better able to accommodate tight framing conditions to reach certain areas of the house. On occasion, flexible ducts serve as branch sections from a main sheet-metal duct, or plenum.

Both sheet metal and flexible duct runs require support along their length. Sagging duct runs not only lead to failures at the joints, but reduce the performance of the forced-air system. And, like plumbing pipes, ducts are generally kept out of the exterior walls to mitigate heat loss through the walls to the outside.

As with the plumbing rough, the home's frame is often designed to accommodate duct runs in and around the structure. In a basement or insulated crawlspace, the duct runs can extend from the furnace (and the air conditioner) directly to the registers cut into the floor above; a chase (or two) can carry a main duct to higher floors of the house and branch out to reach each room.

Lingo:

plenum—a closed chamber between the ductwork and the heating or cooling appliance that regulates the flow of air.

TAKE NOTE: Other heating systems

These days, it's rare to see an oil-powered boiler or a steam-driven system in a new house; even baseboard heating (small electric heaters located and individually controlled in each room) is no longer popular. Freestanding, fuel-burning stoves and fireplaces, while somewhat romantic, are also generally inefficient systems to heat an entire house. In fact, environmental laws restrict the use of fuel-burning (wood) systems in many areas because of their emissions (or exhaust) into the outside air (page 88).

Another alternative energy source, solar, has yet to enter the mainstream. However, passive solar techniques and materials (see sidebar) are likely to be incorporated into new homes more so than active, or mechanical, solar devices.

One system gaining some popularity is in-floor heating systems. Hollow plastic tubes are woven into the floor structure, perhaps set in a grooved section of sheathing, then covered with more sheathing or a lightweight concrete mix. The tubes are filled with heated water, which radiates up through the sheathing or concrete, warming that area of the house.

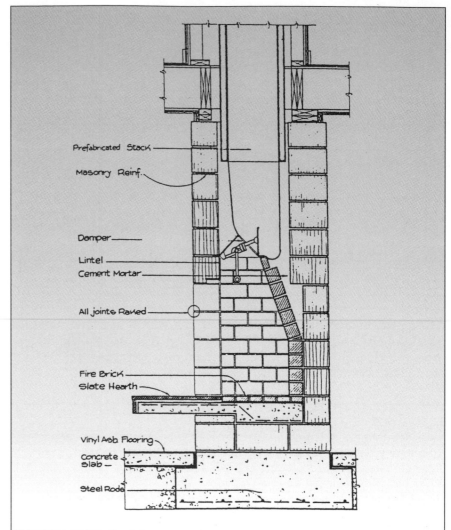

Prefabricated Stack
Masonry Reinf.
Damper
Lintel
Cement Mortar
All joints Raked
Fire Brick
Slate Hearth
Vinyl Asb. Flooring
Concrete Slab
Steel Rods

The guts of a masonry or site-built fireplace, a dying breed in new housing.

From: *Dwelling House Construction*

Most ducts must travel through the home's structure. In a slab-on-grade home, the ductwork generally fits within framed vertical and horizontal chases or within the roof trusses. Occasionally, as with electrical wires and plumbing pipes, the center of wood I-joists can be cut to accommodate a duct run, thus eliminating chases that otherwise might intrude on the interior space in the form of a lower ceiling or at a corner. I-joist manufacturers are very specific about where and how big such cuts can be, though they are often larger than you might imagine.

Photo: Kevin Berne

Increasingly, pre-built fireplaces are used in new housing, though they still require a dedicated vent or flue.

Ventilation

Most HVAC work focuses on the heating and cooling aspects of a given system, but ventilation is an increasing concern, as well. Historically, ventilation focused primarily on the return-air registers to exhaust stale air. Even then, the structure of the house served as a passive ventilator, allowing air to transfer (or "change") via natural pressure differences between indoors and outdoors.

But modern construction techniques and new methods for conserving energy in homes have tightened the building envelope, closing

Lingo:

return-air register—the vent and ductwork used to exhaust air from a room or area and either exhaust it from the house or return it to the HVAC system to be recycled.

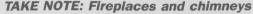

> **TAKE NOTE: Fireplaces and chimneys**
>
> As new and more efficient HVAC systems evolved, the fireplace lost its practicality as a heating appliance. Environmental laws regulating emissions from wood-burning appliances, including fireplaces, has further eroded their popularity and use. And the chimney's role as a cause of heat loss has fallen victim to energy-saving measures and methods.
>
> Rarely, in fact, do new homes have a wood-burning fireplace. Rather, the romanticism of the flame is often expressed in sealed, clean-burning, natural gas units featuring elaborate hearths and multi-sided faces with, on occasion, some heat-generating feature.
>
> Today's fireplaces also relieve a bevy of cumbersome framing details required to protect a wood structure from igniting. An increasing number are "direct vent" units, in which the flue can be vented behind the unit through an exterior wall rather than exhausted vertically through the roof. From the outside, the hooded pipe looks similar to the vent for the clothes dryer.
>
> If, however, your new home is to include a wood-burning fireplace with a vertical chimney, the framing must address the potential fire hazard. To do so, the fire box and flue are constructed of masonry blocks and built at least 2 inches away from any combustible material (the wood framing). The resulting void is often filled with a noncombustible insulation material to retard heat transfer from the fireplace to the structure. On the roof, the top of the chimney must be at least 2 feet above the highest point of the building within a 10-foot radius and be fitted with a spark arrester—a hood that extinguishes sparks and embers before they can get on to the roof and perhaps start a fire.
>
> The construction of a masonry fire box, flue and chimney requires a separate inspection by the building department.

off many of avenues for passive air changes to occur (more on that in Chapter 5). Thus, stale and moist air can become trapped, creating a potential health hazard, mostly allergies and colds.

Builders who promote energy-efficient homes often provide a balanced ventilation system; that is, mechanically exhausting an amount of air equal to what comes into the house via the furnace and air conditioner.

Like the furnace's capacity, ventilation rates are calculated by the size and design of the home and the capacity of the heating and cooling equipment. The system may include a whole-house vent, or, more commonly, a series of "localized" vents in key areas, such as the bathroom, kitchen (via a range hood fan), the garage (for car

What About Solar?

Anyone old enough to remember the oil crisis of the mid-1970s probably recalls the attention paid at the time to finding alternative sources of energy. Among the options, solar appeared to be the most promising. Since the initial hoopla, however, solar has quietly continued to develop as a viable home-energy source, splintering into passive techniques and active, or mechanical, products.

Passive solar heating operates on the premise that certain building materials, properly positioned to capture the sun's heat, collect and evenly distribute that heat in the house.

The use of concrete and masonry is therefore common in passive solar homes because these materials are most effective in storing heat. As the indoor air cools in winter, the heat escapes at an even, albeit uncontrolled, rate. Depending on the amount of solar heat gain desired or relied upon in a house, concrete or masonry is used as the primary structural material, or simply in the foundation slab, fireplace, the exterior finish (brick or stucco) or even a tile floor.

Passive solar, in fact, is part of every home at some level, even if it is unplanned. The most common materials used in a home—namely wood for framing and exterior finishes, asphalt composition roofing and windows—serve in some capacity to transfer heat into the house. Wood has natural insulating qualities, while windows allow both solar heat gain and ventilation.

While passive solar can be quite subtle, makers of active solar systems struggle with not only market acceptance, but the practicality and aesthetics of their products. Unlike passive solar, active solar creates a mechanical system that collects the sun's heat and transforms it into electricity, which, in turn, feeds the furnace and air conditioning units or heat pump, as well as the electrical system and products.

Historically, solar collectors (photovoltaic panels) have been perceived as ugly and intrusive, thus derailing any widespread market success. Newer collectors, formed to replicate common roofing shingles, address those aesthetic concerns but are still too expensive for most new homes. Meanwhile, homeowners remain wary about the reliability of a solar-powered system, despite their proven efficiency.

exhaust) and the attic (where heat and moisture can build up). Local ventilation also includes dedicated ventilation for certain appliances, such as the furnace or clothes dryer. Whole-house vents often operate automatically, while localized vents are mostly controlled by the homeowner.

Localized ventilation focuses on exhausting moist, warm air. Moisture vapor is not only a potential health risk, but if left uncontrolled can eventually rot components of the building structure, degrade insulation and damage windows, doors and other finishes.

Raised consciousness about ventilation as a truly equal member of the HVAC acronym has led to an offshoot industry regarding overall indoor "comfort" and pollutant-free environments. Products such as electronic touch-pad thermostats, humidifiers and dehumidifiers, heat exchangers, air cleaners and other filters can, if properly considered, combine with the basic HVAC equipment to deliver a more comfortable indoor environment. So, too, can the selection of certain windows to reduce glare and heat gain, and reflective barriers that block or trap heat to maintain a more even temperature (see Chapter 5).

Indoor comfort experts also claim energy savings and a healthier lifestyle for the home's occupants, but neither attribute is clear-cut or guaranteed. In fact, even with all the planning and gizmos in the world, the bottom line for the efficient operation of the HVAC system and the comfort of the indoor environment rests with you, the homeowner, and your lifestyle choices. ■

5

Prefinishes

Photo: Kevin Berne

Builders use a variety of materials and systems to create a thermal envelope and provide substrates for finishes such as roofing and siding.

Before we get into the meat of this chapter, it should be made clear that the term "prefinishes" is not a universally used or understood term in the home-building industry. Rather, the steps covered in this chapter—chiefly insulation, windows and doors and drywall—are most often referred to by building professionals as individual steps during construction.

Still, these and associated steps at this point in the building process act in similar capacities; that is, as transitions between the rough stages of construction and the finishes and details of a completed house. Drywall or gypsum panels, for instance, serve not only to cover and protect the rough framing and mechanical systems, but act as a substrate for finishes such as paint, wallpaper and ceramic tile.

In addition, all of these steps are part of what is commonly called the home's thermal envelope; that is, the protection of the interior,

Lingo:

drywall—sheets or panels of pressed gypsum encased in paper; used to create interior wall surfaces.

substrate—a backing for something else, such as paneling, ceramic tile or laminate.

Photo: Rich Binsacca

Exterior sheathing for the exterior walls and roof is among the first "prefinishes" applied.

livable space from outside elements. Insulation, for example, is a key medium for reducing the amount of heat that flows through the walls. Similarly, windows have thermal value and also provide ventilation.

If this were a book about how to hang drywall or install insulation, the steps contained here would certainly deserve their own chapters. Because this book serves to unveil the entire building process, we've grouped these transitional trades and materials in one place under the term "prefinishes."

Lingo:

wall cavity—the space between two wall studs.

Insulation/thermal envelope

Approx. time (days):....2-3
Cum. time (days):....36-49

Insulation

Once the rough mechanicals are installed, the exterior walls are insulated to retard, if not completely block, the transfer of heat within the exterior wall cavities. Few insulation products reduce the flow of air through a wall. Rather, insulation traps the heat carried by that air through the structure (by virtue of pressure differences due to climate, or gaps and cracks in the home's frame). Other products, also covered here, serve to reduce airflow and moisture, and as a result, allow the insulation to be more effective. In turn, the less heat that's allowed to either enter the house (in summer) or escape (in winter) reduces demand on the HVAC system, which therefore reduces the amount of energy used and the cost to purchase that energy.

In house construction, every surface that is exposed to the outside is insulated, including the exterior walls, attic floor, rafters or other roof frame and any floor built over an unheated space, such as a crawlspace or raised wood floor over an unfinished basement. Interior walls are insulated only rarely, and then to reduce noise transfer from one room or area of the house to another. (Sound abatement is an additional benefit of certain kinds of insulation products.)

In addition, interior walls are often cluttered with the pipes and wires of the rough mechanicals, whereas exterior walls may have but a single wiring run intruding on the framed cavity (see Chapter 4). That happy coincidence allows easier and more complete installation of the insulation, especially products that are rolled out, cut and stuffed into the framing, because insulation works best when it is at its full, intended thickness.

Lingo:

sound abatement—the reduction of sound waves through a structure.

A fully sheathed home is ready for windows, doors and exterior finishes.

Photo: Rich Binsacca

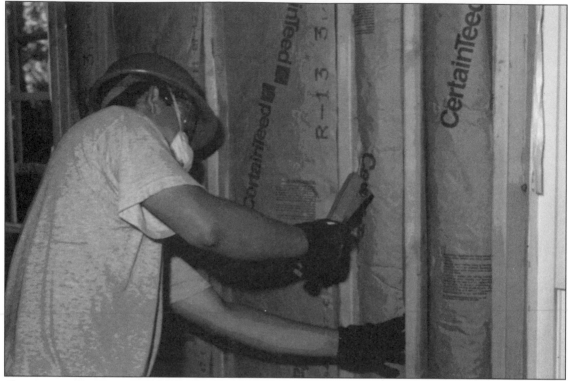

Photo: CertainTeed

The most common wall cavity insulation is fiber glass batts with a protective layer of kraft paper.

R-Value

The effectiveness of insulation is measured by its R-value, or resistance to heat flow at a certain thickness. The thicker the insulation, the higher the R-value and the better its performance. A major reason some builders construct their exterior walls of 2x6s instead of narrower 2x4s (see Chapter 3) is to accommodate a thicker layer of insulation.

Local building codes and the national Model Energy Code (MEC) set standards for the recommended R-value to be placed in walls, top-level ceilings (or attic spaces) and elsewhere, if appropriate, based on climate conditions in certain areas of the country. Codes regulating a heating market like Minnesota require more insulation in a typical house than a moderate climate like Tennessee. Very warm climates, such as the desert Southwest, also require insulation to address wide temperature swings from cool evenings to midday heat. Occasionally, however, such homes may be designed and built to take advantage of passive solar techniques (see Chapter 4) to maintain an even temperature and indoor humidity.

Batts

The prevailing insulation used in new housing is glass fiber, or fiber glass (now generic, but actually a brand name). For vertical surfaces, such as walls, the fibers are formed into 15-inch-wide rolled sections called batts—dry, spongy, airy mats of material. One side of the batt is protected by kraft paper, about the color, texture and thickness of a paper grocery bag, which serves as a backing for the insulation and can provide additional thermal benefits. Paper flaps extending from the sides of the batt may be used to help staple the insulation to wall studs, between floor joists on the underside of a floor structure, or to angled areas, like the roof rafters.

Batts also can be rolled out onto horizontal surfaces, such as in the ceiling. But for that application, many builders rely instead on loose-fill fiber glass, which is essentially dry glass fibers (which look like cotton) blown through a hose into the unused or unfinished attic space.

In the attic, blown-in or loose-fill insulation is a common choice for new homes.

Photo: CertainTeed

93

Photo: Johns Manville Corporation

Under-floor insulation, used above crawlspaces, basements and garages, can reduce heating bills and make the floors of the spaces above much more comfortable.

Loose-fill

Loose-fill insulation provides more complete coverage than rolled batts between the rafters or trusses. Whereas batts allow the wood framing to remain exposed (and therefore conduct heat or cold), a blown-in product covers the wood and also works its way into the nooks and crannies of the framing better than batts.

On rare occasions, you may see loose-fill insulation being installed on the walls, held in the cavity by a thin mesh that is pre-attached to the framing. The cost and time to attach the mesh and blow in the insulation often outweighs the benefits of a loose-fill application on a vertical surface and its superior ability to achieve complete coverage around any intrusions. As such, most builders put batts in the walls and loose-fill in the ceiling.

Cellulose

A small number of home builders are also turning to cellulose, a wet version of the blown-in application, to achieve complete insulating value in the walls without having to first attach a mesh.

Cellulose insulation, made from recycled newspaper and other pulp goods mixed with an adhesive bonding agent, is blown into the wall cavities wet, allowing it accommodate any intrusions in the wall and to stick and dry in place. It's a messy process, especially when the excess cellulose is scraped away flush to the wall studs. Fortunately, the excess material is put back in the hopper for use elsewhere in the house or on another project.

TAKE NOTE: Airflow

Controlling airflow is a key element in reducing energy use and costs. However, it also can take away the ability of the house structure to passively exhaust and refresh indoor air. As we use our homes—the furnace, the gas stove, the shower—we generate moisture and other indoor "pollutants." If they aren't removed, these indoor air hazards can result in mold growth and other allergens, which can impact our health and overall comfort.

Therefore, builders who take measures to reduce airflow also make accommodations to actively (or mechanically) remove stagnant air and replace it with fresh air as part of a comprehensive HVAC system (see Chapter 4).

Injected Foam

Before the wall studs are covered by drywall (see p. 116) or another interior wall finish or panel, your builder may inject expanded foam into small cracks or other openings (such as around an incoming utility conduit or between the studs and a window or door jamb) to block the flow of air into the wall cavity. Injected foam comes in an

Cellulose or spray-applied insulation for walls offers more complete coverage, but can be more expensive to install.

Photo: Spray-Applied Cellulose Assn.

aerosol-like can with a long, thin nozzle. Once it reaches the air, the foam (a non-toxic, polymer formula) expands to several times its contained size to completely cover an opening, joint or other point where air might flow from one side of the wall cavity to the other.

Vapor Retarders

In addition to heat transfer and airflow, the third enemy of the thermal envelope is moisture vapor, or airborne moisture. Moisture vapor migrates through the structure from areas of high humidity (such as outdoors on a South Florida summer day) to areas of low humidity (such as inside an air-conditioned house).

To mitigate moisture, and depending on your climate and building codes, your builder may also install a thin layer of continuous plastic sheeting called a vapor retarder. In all cases, a vapor retarder is installed on the "cold side" of the wall. If you live in a cool climate, therefore, the vapor retarder is secured to the exterior sheathing. In a warm climate, it is placed on the inside face of the studs, just before the drywall or other paneling.

When properly installed, a vapor retarder works in conjunction with the insulation and airflow controls to deliver a complete ther-

Photo: Kevin Berne

Lingo:

humidity—the amount of moisture in the air.

Injected or expanding foam insulation helps seal cracks and openings more effectively than fiber glass materials, blocking air infiltration.

Additional Measures

Builders who construct homes that are especially energy-saving, and who market that benefit to distinguish themselves from their competition, may take even more measures to control heat transfer, airflow and moisture.

An increasingly common product—rigid foam panels—replaces exterior sheathing, most commonly at the corners (where the structure is most susceptible to air and heat transfer). These structurally rated panels, measuring the same dimension as the plywood they replace, not only provide adequate lateral support but also a superior insulating value. They also are more lightweight than plywood, can be cut with a knife instead of a power saw and install with the same fasteners, allowing faster construction.

Also on the outside, a builder may install an air barrier that covers the entire length and breadth of the sidewalls (with cut-outs for windows and doors). An air barrier, also called a house wrap, is an extra step in reducing the likelihood of air and wind-driven rain getting into the wall cavities.

The thin, fibrous plastic sheeting of an air barrier is delicately perforated, however, to allow moisture vapor (as opposed to water or rain) and some air to escape from the wall cavity to the outside, thus properly venting the walls should moisture get in. If installed, an air barrier is the last step of the exterior wall construction before the application of the windows, doors and finished siding and trim.

Inside, some builders also install radiant barriers, typically on the underside of the ceiling joists to block (or radiate) heat that rises from the room to the floor or attic above. Radiant barriers are bright, silvery sheets of thin plastic material, which are rolled out and installed with the reflective layer facing the area where heat is to be kept from rising beyond the ceiling.

mal envelope. Combined, these elements keep the wall cavities warm and dry. If moisture does get in through the exterior walls, it is turned away at the vapor retarder before it gets to the insulation, drywall and interior wall finishes, where it can cause damage and even failure. It is then vented out the way it came.

Creating this thermal envelope takes about two or three days for an average-size house, depending on the use of one or all three components per code or your builder's practices and scheduling skill. It also may require an inspection before the insulation is hidden from view.

Today's more efficient windows and doors allow more creative uses.

Photo: Weather Shield Windows & Doors

Windows and Doors

Ever since the completion of framing and installation of the exterior roof and sidewall sheathing, your house doesn't appear to have changed much. Sure, there are folks going in and out every day, all day, but the dramatic progress you saw during framing has slowed considerably while the various mechanical trades and insulation contractors do their jobs. A walk through your house still shows exposed walls, albeit filled with pipes and wires and pink or white matts of insulation. You can still hear the noise from the street, as the workers take their coffee or lunch break.

Window and door installation

Approx. time (days): 3
Cum. time (days):....39-52

That will change soon as the windows and doors are installed. While most folks understand and value the purpose of doors and windows as gateways and viewfinders, few home buyers get to experience or realize their sound-abatement benefits.

Photo: Weather Shield Windows & Doors

Pre-hung window units, now the standard, allow fast and easy installation.

Windows and doors serve several functions in a house. As part of the thermal envelope, they help control heat transfer, moisture and airflow, and are the primary "passive ventilation" method for refreshing the indoor air (once all the gaps and other openings have been sealed). If you shut your windows and blinds on your way out to work in the morning and return home in the heat of the day, you should notice a dramatic difference in temperature between the outdoors and inside the house.

Windows and doors also are among the most exposed and vulnerable products in a house, bearing the brunt of the outdoor elements

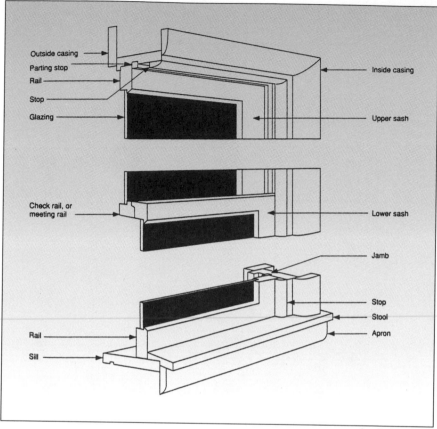

Outside casing
Parting stop
Rail
Stop
Glazing

Inside casing

Upper sash

Check rail, or
meeting rail

Lower sash

Jamb

Stop
Stool
Apron

Rail

Sill

*Elements of a "hung"
window, the most com-
mon type in new housing.*

Caradco/JELD-WEN

(wind, rain, sunlight and heat) and the indoor environment, where excessive moisture can cause condensation and damage on the inside of cheap, poorly constructed windows.

Of course, doors and windows have a direct and obvious functional purpose: to provide access to and from the house, including views. They are a measure of safety and security, too, and provide the home with natural light. Finally, windows and doors are often the showcase features of your home's style, providing drama and excitement from the street and inside, too.

The average new house has three exterior doors (front, rear, and side, including patio or French-style doors, or one to a detached garage), perhaps 20 or more interior doors (between rooms and for bathrooms and closets), one or more garage doors and about 20 windows of various shapes and sizes.

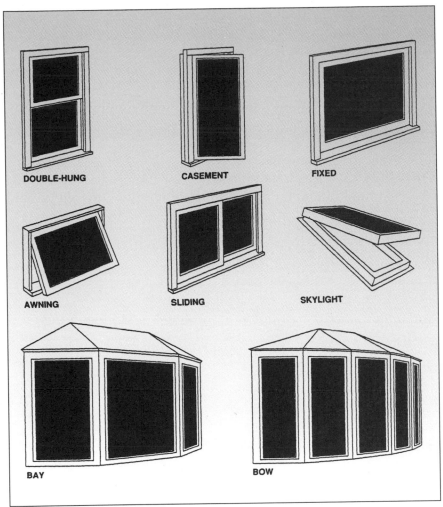

DOUBLE-HUNG   CASEMENT   FIXED

AWNING   SLIDING   SKYLIGHT

BAY   BOW

Caradco/JELD-WEN

Windows are available in a variety of styles, shapes and operating systems.

The placement of windows and doors, if thought through by the architect, designer or builder, considers their multi-functional value. The front door, for instance, may align with a window along the back wall of the house to facilitate airflow as well as provide a direct line of sight (or view) from the front to the rear of the house, delivering a sense of spaciousness and light.

Similarly, windows might be ganged (placed side-by-side) to enclose an east-facing breakfast nook for morning light, while a sliding glass door may be installed in a specific place to catch prevailing breezes and also provide access to a rear deck, patio or yard.

Windows and doors are provided in an almost unending variety of styles, shapes, sizes, operating functions and materials. Of course, there are those styles and types most commonly used: door openings, for instance, are almost always between 30 and 36 inches wide (in builder and door manufacturing lingo, between 2-6 and 3-0, which refers to measurements in feet and inches).

Wood is the prevailing material for both doors and windows, though synthetic and composite products and protective claddings (or covers) made to look like wood are gaining popularity. For windows, casement style (in which the window is hinged on one side and swings out when open) and double-hung or sash windows (which operate up and down) are the most common types used by builders. Doors are either flush (or flat) or decorated with a variety of raised or moulded panels (commonly six, in two vertical rows of three panels).

French doors with stationary panels and a simple grille pattern help break up expansive amounts of glass.

Photo: Weather Shield Windows & Doors

No matter the material, style, shape or any other variation possible, all windows and all doors generally install the same way, respectively.

Windows

All new windows made today are pre-hung; that is, the glass is set and sealed in the jamb (sides) and sash, with a sill and stool (bottom parts) and header (top part) in place. The resulting window "unit" arrives at the job site ready to install. The size and shape are determined beforehand by the building plans, which indicate the rough-frame openings for each unit ordered.

Flashing and calking. Because windows are vulnerable to the outside elements, particularly wind and rain, a material, called flashing, is often installed around the framed opening before the window unit is nailed or secured into place. Flashing can be a left-over section of the air barrier material (see above) or a cut section of roofing paper (or felt; see Chapter 6).

> **TAKE NOTE: Site-built windows**
>
> Before there were factory-built and pre-hung units, windows were built on the job site. For picture or fixed windows (those that don't open), the jamb—the finished "frame" of a window—were nailed to the rough-frame opening. The installer then cut a single pane of glass to fit the opening, and held it in place within the jamb with thin sections of wood and tiny metal triangles, called stops, on either side of the pane's perimeter. The connection between the stops and the glass was then sealed with putty.
>
> Hung or sash windows were much more complicated to build, though the sashes were essentially glazed windows that were then hung by a series of concealed ropes, weights and pulleys within a larger frame to facilitate their operation up and down. A stop was installed along the window sill to hold the bottom sash in place and block air and moisture at that point. Casement and sliding windows were also complicated, and didn't gain widespread acceptance or use until they were made in a factory.

The purpose of flashing is to create a barrier or membrane between the window unit and the rough frame against moisture infiltration and migration. Flashing is installed from the bottom of the opening to the top, so that sections overlap each other in such a way that water cascading down won't get behind the flashing material.

In addition, builders who provide energy-saving homes may also caulk or seal the rough opening before the window is installed. Caulking is a paste-like polymer substance that is squeezed out of a

Lingo:

flashing—protection against water or moisture infiltration, typically around roof protrusions and windows.

tube with a metallic or plastic gun-like tool. A "bead" of caulk is a continuous line of the stuff that, when flattened by the weight and shape of the window, creates yet another seal against water and air between the frame and window unit. Because of its polymer content, caulk remains flexible and thus expands and moves with the window unit to maintain its seal.

> **TAKE NOTE: Caulking**
>
> If the bead of caulk is disturbed before the window is in place, it is generally ineffective. Smeared or flattened beads cannot make the proper bond with the window sash. And, to be clear, caulk is not an adhesive; it provides no structural value at all to hold the window in place.

Window installation. Like other prefinishes, windows are a transition from the rough frame to the finished house. Made under factory conditions and controls, windows have tighter tolerances than the stud wall construction. As such, before they are nailed into the rough openings, windows are often shimmed (like the sill plate, see Chapter 3) so they fit level, plumb and square in the opening.

If the framing is accurate, there's usually minimal shimming of each window—minor adjustments that align it perfectly in the hole provided. If needed, shims can be installed along any edge and from both sides of the window, with the two tapered edges of each shim meeting in the middle of the window's edge between the unit and the rough opening.

Builders or window installers may shim before they caulk the opening, then remove the shims and the window unit, caulk the frame, and then reset the unit and shims. Once they know the placement of the shims, they can replace them in the same location, check for level, plumb and square, and then screw or nail the window into place.

Fastening a window to the frame may occur from the sides into the adjacent framing (through pre-drilled holes in the window unit's sash), or through a factory-applied nailing fin (or flap) that extends from the edges of the window and is held tight against the outside sheathing to accept nails through to the wall studs. Often, the fin is also caulked to guard against moisture infiltration, and may even be flashed at the top before the installation of the exterior finish (siding, brick, stucco, etc.).

Lingo:

nailing fin—a skirt or flap attached to a skylight, roof window, window or roof vent to help secure a product to the structure.

Finally, some builders may take a final step and insulate and seal any gaps between the window unit and the rough opening or adjacent framing. Usually, using sections of fiber glass batt insulation does little good (as the material works best when at its full thickness), but injecting expanded foam insulation to block air gaps is quite effective. One caveat: the foam expands at such a great rate that builders must be careful not to push the unit out of square or level when they inject the foam.

TAKE NOTE: *Window problems*

It seems simple: you have a hole and a window that appears to fit into it. Why so many steps to actually install the unit? In fact, careless or improper installation of windows, while not as dire as a structural flaw, can have far-reaching impacts.

First, and most obvious, the window won't operate freely, often sticking or failing to close tight to the sash. That problem allows uncontrolled air, moisture and thermal transfer, which can lead to condensation problems, mold and mildew and degradation of the window components.

Finishing. Once the window is secured to the frame, many builders will remove the sashes or unhinge the glass portion of a casement or sliding window and set them aside, protecting them from damage. Because today's window glass is more high-tech in its construction, insulating characteristics and components and connection to the sash (see sidebar, "Insulating Glass"), a broken or damaged window can cause delays and extra costs to replace or repair. Fortunately, window makers have adjusted to this reality, creating sashes that are lightweight and easily removed—a feature that also allows both exterior and interior panes to be cleaned more easily.

For the same reason, the window supplier, often a local company, will hold back delivery of the window screens until just before you move in to protect the screen material from on-site damage, as well.

Lingo:

condensation—the formation of water from airborne moisture on a surface when temperature of that surface is below that of the air.

TAKE NOTE: Roof windows and skylights

Skylights and roof windows are units that are installed in the roof frame to provide natural light from above. Increasingly popular in new housing, these units first gained a foothold in the home-improvement industry.

The technical difference between a roof window and a skylight is that the former is operable, or opens for ventilation, while a skylight is fixed or inoperable, providing only light. Like standard windows, both types are "pre-hung," including an integral nailing fin and specially designed flashing material. They are set and secured to the roof framing, just as standard windows are hung in the rough openings of a stud wall.

Flashing is the key element to a successful and reliable skylight or roof window installation. Unlike wall-hung windows (and doors), these units are completely exposed to the weather and water runoff from the roof. Essentially, you are creating a huge hole in your roof that must be protected from water infiltration. Proper flashing around the roof windows and skylights is therefore vital to shed that water away from the intruding windows.

Skylights and roof windows also require additional framing, most noticeably in the attic to create the "channel" that directs the light from the unit through the ceiling. To enclose it, this extra framing is drywalled, taped and finished on the inside (where it can be seen), but usually left unfinished on the outside, as the shaft is seen only if you crawl up into the attic.

Roof windows (shown) and skylights have advanced flashing systems that eliminate leaks when installed properly.

Photo: Kevin Berne

Photo: Kevin Berne

Most doors are pre-hung, as well, though the actual doors are removed from the frame and then reinstalled later to protect them during construction.

Doors

Unlike windows, most doors are still installed the old-fashioned way, by building a frame within the rough opening, cutting for hinges, locks and other hardware, and then "hanging" the door (on its hinges) within the frame. Adjustments for square, plumb and level are easily made to either the door itself (by cutting or planing it) or the frame (with shims) to ensure proper and smooth operation.

Pre-hung doors. Some manufacturers and local door suppliers also offer pre-hung doors for a faster and easier installation. Like window units, pre-hung doors arrive on the job site with everything in place: jamb, hardware, holes for the handle and locks, etc.—based on the plans and specifications (called the "door schedule" listed on the blueprints) provided to the door maker or local supplier by the builder.

Lingo:

planing—the process of creating or forming a flat surface.

107

Photo: Kevin Berne

Patio doors, often with both fixed and operable "panels," combine the benefits of windows and doors.

Pre-hung doors are sold at a premium cost to standard doors, but that's because a lot of the work has already been done. You either pay the door company or the builder's carpenter to install the door, with the total cost often less for a pre-hung unit. Like windows, pre-hung doors are fitted into the rough-frame opening, shimmed if necessary, and screwed or nailed from the side jamb into the adjacent studs.

The jamb also provide a "stop" or edge for the drywall or other paneling to butt into, as well as a nailing surface for the interior casing or trim that often surrounds door and window openings to finish them off.

Whether pre-hung or site-installed, doors are available in several styles, material compositions and sizes. Most are rated for their fire resistance, expressed in terms of the minutes it would take a fire to breach the door. Some doors, like those to a closet or bathroom, typically require no fire rating. Codes often dictate a particular rating for doors between an attached garage and the living space, at an entry or to a bedroom, as a precaution against house fires and to help ensure occupant safety.

Styles. Of all the styles of doors, regardless of their construction (solid wood, steel, fiber glass, composite veneer, among others), the two main categories are flush and panel. Flush doors are flat and plain, and most often used in affordable or low-cost homes, as utility doors, or dressed up with glass inserts or attached trim moulding to create a more stylish and dimensional look. By contrast, panel (or raised-panel) doors feature a pattern set into or protruding out from the door surface.

Before doors were made in a factory, panel doors showcased a carpenter's skill. Even in today's sterile conditions, true panel doors are put together much the same way as their historic counterparts.

To mitigate shrinkage and expansion in seasonal climate changes, solid wood panel doors are made of several smaller components fitted together. Within the basic perimeter frame of stiles and

Entry doors have become focal points with the use of sidelites and other decorative elements.
Photo: Kevin Berne

Lingo:

stiles—on a panel door or cabinet front, the horizontal members of the panel frame.

TAKE NOTE: Construction doors

Because the entry door is often the most ornate and expensive door in the house (not counting the cost of the garage doors), many suppliers and builders first install a "construction door" in its place until just before you move in or inspect the house before closing escrow.

A construction door is typically a flush, unfinished and relatively cheap unit that is installed to take the abuse of the myriad subcontractors traipsing through to complete the interior. It serves to enclose and secure the house, and spares the true entry door from damage and costly repairs or refinishing.

Lingo:

rails—on a panel door or cabinet front, the vertical sides of the panel frame.

A panel (or "raised panel") door is still often made from a combination of individual components, allowing for expansion and contraction during changes in climate.

rails, the raised panels are fitted loosely to allow slight movement and shifting in varying climate conditions, thus guarding against the entire door warping or racking (getting out of square). A warped door is hard to close or open, rubs against the jamb or shifts it so that the lock no longer aligns with its hole.

With composite doors, manufacturers simply mould or impress a pattern on a pressed-wood or rigid foam core and then laminate a wood-grained veneer on that pattern to simulate a raised-panel door. Composite doors are lighter in weight, accept and hold paints and stains, and are often better insulators than solid wood doors. They're also less expensive and require less upkeep.

For most new subdivision homes, the builder will install a solid wood, steel or moulded fiber glass entry door, perhaps with matching long, thin windows (called sidelites) on one or both sides for added style.

Inside, the doors are most likely moulded composite doors, while a fire-rated door to the garage might be made of steel. In lower-

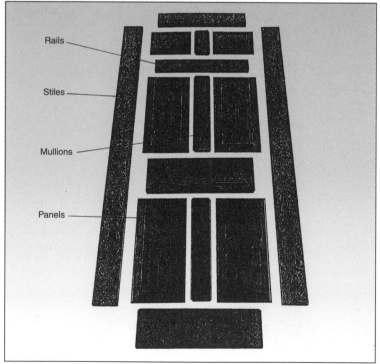

Rails

Stiles

Mullions

Panels

Morgan Door/ JELD-WEN

priced homes, moulded steel entry doors, with an insulating core, are common because of their affordable price and easy maintenance, though they do tend to dent easily.

The hybrid of windows and doors are patio doors, either sliding or French-style. Both types are mostly glass to allow views and provide natural light, but they also provide door-like access to the outdoors. The difference is their operation, either on a track (sliding) or hinged (French or casement). Additionally, some sections (or panels) may be fixed or inoperable, lending themselves exclusively as windows, albeit from the floor to just below the ceiling.

Patio doors are installed similarly to other doors and windows, can be shipped pre-hung or not and provide both functional and aesthetic value. Their weight and size, however, often requires additional structural support (primarily a larger header) if the opening is more than five feet across, which is accommodated in the plans and built during rough framing.

TAKE NOTE: Mullions

Time was when windows and glass doors were made with integrated mullions—thin, moulded pieces of wood that created a gridded pattern on the glass. The glass sections of the pattern were and still are called "lites," and until the industrial age of window-making, each lite was a separately glazed unit. When a lite broke, you simply cut another piece of glass to fit and reglazed it in place.

Today, what's now known as "true divided lite" (or TDL) windows replicate the individually glazed mullion patterns of the past. But more commonly in new homes, windows either have no mullions at all, or the pattern is created by a separate grid that is attached to the outside of the glass. In some cases, the grid pattern is held between two panes of insulating glass. Often, depending on when you buy the home and its state of completion, you may be able to ask for a specific grille pattern before the windows are ordered or shipped.

One primary reason for attached or in-pane grilles is cleaning. Remove a grille (which often looks like a tic-tac-toe board) from the outside of a window, and you can wash the entire pane of glass without having to work around the mullions. In-pane grids are even easier, as they rest between the two inside faces of the glass, leaving the exposed surfaces smooth.

Cost also has a lot to do with the use of attached and in-pane grille patterns. TDL windows are expensive, often a custom or special order, and reglazing is a lost art. If a pane breaks in a modern-day TDL window, the complicated gasketing and sealant system that holds it in the sash makes it as expensive to replace as a full-size window.

Morgan Door/ JELD-WEN

Morgan Door/ JELD-WEN

Factory-moulded garage doors (above) and interior doors (right) offer a higher level of style to production homes.

Garage Doors

Garage doors are often the forgotten products in this stage of construction, if only because they lack the sophistication and complexity of windows and passage doors. In fact, garage doors are often the first doors installed, thereby creating a secure and enclosed storage area for the builder's tools, materials and other products to be applied later.

Garage doors are available in standard two-door width and in single-door styles, depending on the design of the garage openings. Almost all garage doors today are sectional across their width (horizontally), which allows them to roll up along metal tracks and hug the ceiling of the garage, out of the way of cars and kids.

Most are made of steel, and may be prefinished or simply shipped with a prime coat and finished (painted) on the job site. Other variations are of composites (fiber glass, engineered wood) or other synthetics. In most cases, the garage door supplier will send an installer to hang the door, hook up the automatic opener and check its operation.

Hardware

The final step in door (and window) installation is the hardware—the myriad locks, handles, pulls, cranks and other accessories that complete a unit's function and form. Most of today's factory-built wood windows and doors are routed (or cut) for the installation of hardware; others have the metal pieces already in place.

Insulating Glass

Most windows built before 1980 or so were single-pane; that is, only one pane (or layer) of glass was set in the sash between the outside and the home's interior. These windows were notorious for conducting cold air and allowing uncontrolled airflow through the unit (especially at the glazed glass-to-sash connection). In terms of thermal value, a window wasn't much better than an open hole in the wall.

The energy crisis of the mid-'70s and research into home-energy use prompted the introduction of dual-pane and insulating glass technology. It is now standard for all new windows to have at least two panes of glass, with a much more sophisticated connection between the glass and the sash to reduce airflow.

But simply doubling the amount of glass wasn't enough. Windows of the last decade often feature transparent films that reflect heat, while an inert and invisible gas, heavier than air, reduces thermal transfer between the panes. As the insulating quality (also expressed as R-value, like insulation) rises, however, so does the cost of the window.

The Model Energy Code, and perhaps your local building department, may require a minimum R-value for windows and glass patio doors or limit the number of windows you can install to help reduce energy use and solar heat gain. Otherwise, it's up to you or the builder to decide how energy efficient you want (or need) your windows and glass doors to be, and at what price.

Time Frame

The time it takes to install doors and windows depends on the number of units being hung and their size, shape and placement. A simple double-hung unit in a bedroom takes about 20-30 minutes, including flashing, caulking and shimming. A two-story-high picture window set into a living room wall may take a few hours. Assuming an average house with a typical door and window schedule, it should take a pair of carpenters or the dealer's installers about three days to put in the windows and doors.

While some windows and doors are regulated by code (for egress and fire rating), a separate inspection for window and door installation is typically unnecessary. Rather, the building department will check egress and fire-rated doors, if required, upon final inspection before issuing a Certificate of Occupancy (see Chapter 8).

Photo: Kevin Berne

Drywall panels are delivered in stacks for faster and easier installation.

Drywall

Like the exterior sheathing, drywall (also called gypsum board or Sheetrock, a brand name) serves to enclose the wall, this time on the interior side. Drywall also completes the thermal envelope, hides the rough framing, mechanicals and insulation, serves as a fire barrier, and provides a flat, smooth substrate for finishes like paint and wallpaper.

Also, like the plywood used as sheathing over the rough frame, drywall is a product of the industrial age of home building. Made and shipped in panels measuring 4 feet wide by 8, 10 or 12 feet high and usually ½-inch thick, drywall (or pressed gypsum, a naturally occurring material) replaced the cumbersome lath-and-plaster system of interior wall and ceiling construction. Today, drywall panels are easily cut to fit any two-dimensional shape and nailed or screwed in place within minutes, reducing the built-up lath-and-plaster method to one simple step.

Lingo:

Sheetrock—a brand name for drywall manufactured by United States Gypsum (USG) Corporation.

lath-and-plaster—the process for creating interior walls before the invention and use of drywall in which thin strips of wood were attached to the wall studs and covered with a thin layer of plaster, which then dried to the finished surface. Gaps left between the lath helped secure the plaster to the wall.

114

TAKE NOTE: Curved drywall

How do you drywall a curved wall or the arched opening to a window or door? When builders used lath and plaster, it was easy to nail thin sections of lath and apply the wet plaster to conform to any shape, even the tightest radius. But a ½-inch-thick panel of drywall doesn't bend very easily.

In most contoured cases, builder or drywall contractors turn to thinner panels, usually ¼-inch. At that thickness, the drywall is more easily bent. The installer simply doubles the layers to create ½-inch thick coverage (often dictated by code for fire protection). In tighter conditions, the initial drywall installation may show several, squared-off joints of several, smaller pieces used to make a tight turn, which are then smoothed out by the joint compound and texturing steps to create the curve or arch.

Drywall panels are encased in thin paper—a dirty white color on the exposed edges with a lesser-grade, gray paper backing. The paper contains and protects the pressed gypsum, which is easily broken apart and disintegrates in water. The thin paper layer and soft composition of drywall make it easy to cut or saw to fit any application.

Easily cut and shaped around the structural frame, drywall provides the substrate for interior finishes.

Photo: Kevin Berne

Drywall installation
Approx. time (days):....3-4
Cum. time (days):....42-56

Drywall Installation

Drywall is perhaps the one "prefinish" stage of construction that takes the longest and shows the least progress in its time frame—foreshadowing the finishing phases that follow. While drywall panels are relatively easy to manipulate and put in place, the numerous joints between the panels and the divots made for nails or screws must be filled and smoothed out to create a flat, seamless surface for the eventual wall and ceiling finishes.

The first phase, hanging the drywall, takes the average three-person crew about three or four days to complete; less so on simply designed homes or with more crew members. Most drywall panels need to be cut to accommodate window and door openings, corners, arches and other features, which adds time.

The panels also need to be nailed or screwed to the home's frame, with the edges of two panels often sharing a narrow stud. Where there is no stud or other structural member for securing the edge of a panel, some manufacturers offer metal clips that stabilize the drywall in place. The nailing pattern for drywall is typically six inches between nails or screws along the perimeter of each panel and eight inches with the "field" of each panel—a pattern that will be inspected by the building department.

Once the drywall is hung in place, however, the interior of your home takes on a more realistic appearance. No longer are you distracted by views through wall studs, now blocked by the drywall. You get a real, tangible sense of the width of your hallways and door openings, and a clearer idea about where furniture and artwork might go to cover these blank walls.

Unfortunately, if you visit the house again within a week or so, not much will have changed that you'll immediately notice. The next two phases of drywall installation, tape and texture, are slow-moving. Simply, the wet compound (or "mud"), used to bridge the joints between drywall panels, cover fasteners and create finished corners, needs to dry, be sanded and re-applied a few times before the walls are adequately smooth and seamless.

Mudding, Taping and Texturing

The initial mudding and taping of joints, fasteners and corners takes about a day, perhaps two. Thin strips of paper are set into a swath of joint compound along the length of each panel connection as a bridge to mitigate cracks and then are screed (or pressed tightly along its length) against the mud base, securing it across the joint

Lingo:

screed—the smoothing of a concrete surface, also called strikeoff.

Photo: Kevin Berne

It takes several steps (and days) to hide drywall joints and fasteners to create a smooth, surface.

and squeezing the excess to either side of the tape. The excess is then scraped off and used later, perhaps on the next joint or corner.

At corners, sections of thin sheet metal, moulded into sharp or curved corners (called corner bead), are nailed into the framing, then covered over by the joint compound to hide the connection.

Once completed, this stage of drywall is allowed to dry for a day. Occasionally, especially where a thick coat of compound was required, you might see small cracks in the drying mud. Not to worry; such cracks will be filled by the next layer of joint compound.

Once dry, the mud is sanded smooth (a dusty, messy process that pervades every nook and cranny of the house), and wiped clean to eliminate any dust particles on the drywall. That step alone can take a full day or more, including clean-up, in preparation for the next layer of mud.

Drywall tape and texture (2X)
Approx. time (days):....4-5
Cum. time (days):....46-61

117

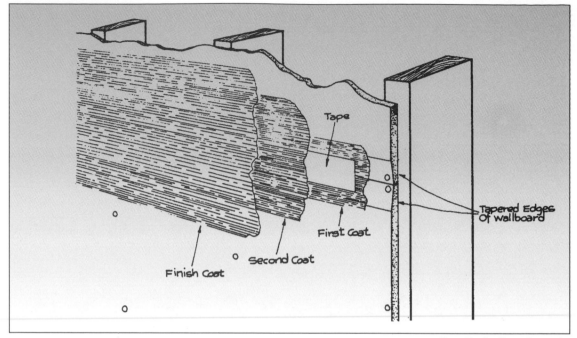

Tape

First Coat

Second Coat

Finish Coat

Tapered Edges Of Wallboard

From: *Dwelling House Construction*

The basic steps of drywall finishing; expect a day or more between each step to allow for adequate drying and sanding.

Subsequent layers of joint compound, each progressively thinner, are needed to "float out" or flatten any areas of the wall surface that aren't smooth or flush to the rest of the wall. How many layers depends on the construction of the walls and the initial drywall installation. No matter how many, each application of joint compound must be allowed to dry thoroughly and be sanded and wiped down before the next layer. Count on at least two days for each "cycle" of joint compound application. However, the thinner the layer, the less times it takes to dry, perhaps just overnight.

In many cases, the last step of drywall installation is texturing. Generically, texturing refers to the progressive steps toward a smooth wall (i.e., floating). But it also refers to adding a last layer once the wall is smooth and seamless. In that case, the builder or drywall contractor may add dimension to the wall or ceiling using a thinner mixture of joint compound to give the surface the look of a brushed or sweeping stucco, tiny bumps or pimples (called stipples), or some other texture.

Dimensioned or smooth, when the walls are deemed ready for finish they don't appear to look much different than just after the initial drywall installation—a step that may have occurred a week ago or more. Get used to that feeling as the house nears completion.

TAKE NOTE: Backer board

Though drywall is the prevailing interior wall substrate in new homes, it does not stand up well to water or moisture. In fact, the use of a vapor retarder behind it serves to protect the drywall from moisture that might make its way from the outside, thus mitigating the chance of moldy streaks on the exposed surface of the panels or wall finish.

Where ceramic tile or some other wet-set finish is to be applied to a wall or ceiling (in a shower or tub enclosure, along the back of a countertop or for a brick-veneer fireplace), standard gypsum board is inadequate. In some cases, codes mandate a more moisture-resistant substrate to ensure the integrity of the wall and the finish.

A popular choice in those circumstances is called backer board, a fiber-reinforced gypsum panel with a heavier grade of moisture-resistant paper backing. Also called green board because of its color, backer board provides the stability for tile and similar material applications. The panels not only block moisture, but are stronger, allowing them to carry the extra weight of a wall or ceiling of dense ceramic tile or stone, plus the weight of the mortar and grout needed to apply the finish.

Paneling

Few materials encompass the multi-functional value of drywall as an interior wall and ceiling substrate (remember, the floor is plywood). Wood or composite paneling may be applied directly to the studs, but it often lacks the thermal, fire and sound abatement qualities of drywall.

And, if paneling is unprotected by a vapor retarder or left unfinished on its hidden side and edges, it can buckle, peel or de-laminate with moisture gain from the wall cavity. Most paneling, in fact, is installed over a layer of drywall, chiefly to maintain an adequate fire barrier.

Drywall and paneling manufacturers may offer gypsum panels with a moulded pattern, which allows the builder to gain the efficiencies and value of drywall, but with a built-in style and dimension. Stamped metal also is an alternative, though most of those products also are applied over the drywall.

Whether wood, metal, or gypsum, however, paneling is an aesthetic risk for a tract builder, many of whom are trying to sell homes to the broadest audience possible (within a certain demographic, like young families or seniors). Even the most elegant or simple paneling pattern might turn off a segment of the target market.

Better to let you, the buyer, ask for or add paneling in the extra bedroom or a wainscot in the dining room. Unless the builder is constructing huge, luxury spec homes that demand all the trimmings, he or she saves money and time by providing blank, painted walls and minimal trim, casings and other finishes (see Chapter 7) until the buyer chooses them before closing or adds them after the sale.

At this point, with the drywall hung and textured, the doors and windows installed and the thermal envelope enclosed, your new house is ready for finishes. The dramatic, three-dimensional progress you've witnessed through much of the process so far will, from now on, come in mere glimpses, such as when the kitchen cabinets and appliances are installed, or when the windows are trimmed out and painted. Most of the time, because of the volume of finishes and meticulous nature in which they are applied, the steps toward completion of your house is a slow-moving process. ■

Lingo:

spec homes—homes that are designed and built on the prospect of being sold during construction or upon completion, or on the "speculation" of an eventual buyer.

Exterior Finishes

Photo: Rich Binsacca

A famliar scene: unopened packages of roofing await an installation crew. The actual application takes about two days.

With the thermal envelope closed up, the process of finishing your new home begins. For several reasons, this last stage of construction—the application of both exterior and interior finishes—seems to take the longest. Ironically, it's when everyone is counting the days to completion and patience for any glitch is running low.

This phase is also when you, as a homeowner, are most involved in the process, and, therefore, more apt to pay closer attention, find flaws and be relied upon to make more decisions that impact time, quality and budget. While you may have chosen the color of the siding and your appliances long ago, now is when they are delivered to the job site and installed. If you bought the house after construction began, you may be able to swap a few specifications regarding the finishes. However, making any changes at this point can lead to a drawn-out schedule, extra cost and added stress.

Photo: Kevin Berne

Felt, or building paper, is a basic flashing material under the roofing finish, helping shed and block water away from the wood sheathing.

But it's also your responsibility to catch mistakes in the ordering of products, and demand they be corrected. In large subdivisions, especially, when several homes are being built at the same time by the same builder, errors can happen. Try to treat these hiccups as honest mistakes. Remember, no builder wants to purposely spend any more time than necessary completing a house. Know, too, that most conventional finishes are purchased through local suppliers, allowing mistakes or revised orders to be handled more quickly.

While it is common to have carpenters and subcontractors finishing the exterior and interior simultaneously, we'll start with the outside. Exterior finishes typically include the roofing, siding, trim, lighting and gutters. The application of other features and products, such as pathways, patios, fences, site drainage and various items of landscaping, are often dictated by the contract or by requirements placed on the builder as part of the marketing or covenants of the overall development.

In some cases, simply delivering the finished house, with a driveway, a walk up to the front door and some front-yard sod, is all some builders do. Additional landscaping, fencing and other auxiliary features are either extra or left up to you, the homeowner.

Lingo:

covenants—the rules of a community governing such things as landscape design, features and maintenance, house color and other items that impact the overall value of the neighborhood or community.

sod—sections of grass or turf rolled out to create a lawn or other ground-cover.

Roofing

There are several types of roofing material used on new single-family homes, from slate and Mission-style tiles to cedar shingles and

Choosing Finishes

Why and how does a builder choose the finishes for a house, especially one sold on speculation, with no specific buyer helping call the shots? As business people, builders take a very practical and strategic approach to creating homes that will appeal to the type of buyers they hope to attract.

The first consideration is cost. A builder's profit is made primarily on a fast sale from a properly priced or market-rate home and his or her markup on the products used to build and finish the house. Less expensive products mean fewer dollars spent (a penny saved ...), but sometimes a builder will use a more expensive product or brand name with extra value that he or she can sell for a higher profit.

With that, the cost to install certain products also works into the equation. The use of cheap products that are difficult or time-consuming to apply is common in home building only because some builders fail to consider installed costs versus initial costs. Savvy builders, however, are more likely to choose a combination of price and installation to strike a balance. Those that consider long-term value and performance will also factor in a product's warranty or service package, which may save time and money after the home is completed.

Beyond costs, builders also might take into account a product's performance or durability, especially in extreme climates. Market acceptance of a product also comes to mind, as builders generally bow to public consensus and are hesitant to take fashion risks or otherwise limit their selling appeal with non-traditional features and finishes.

A finish product's appearance is often the last consideration, if at all part of the equation. Certainly, builders want their homes to look good. But builders know that "beauty" in the eyes of most home buyers often has more to do with price and location than any aesthetic feature. An unspectacular home that is priced right and in a desirable neighborhood will outsell a trimmed-out house in a less desirable location.

even plastic panels. The choice is dictated by regional preferences, the design of the house and other finishes and occasionally the building code.

Before any actual roofing goes on, however, a few critical steps need to take place. The first is a layer of roofing paper, which serves to protect the sheathing and provide a moisture and water barrier between the frame and the finished roofing material. Black and stiff, roofing paper (or "felt") is rolled out in continuous lengths parallel to the edge, or eave, of the roof. Starting at the eaves, subsequent courses overlap the previous layer so that water cascading down the roof slope won't get under the felt.

Lingo:

installed costs—the price of a product plus the cost to install it.

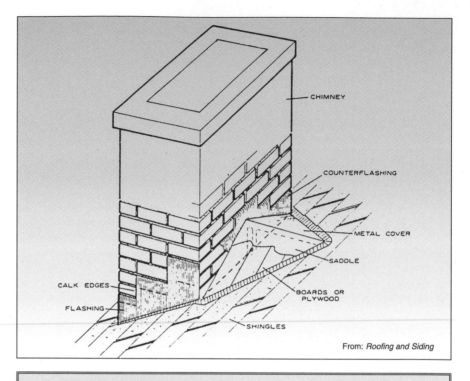

CHIMNEY

COUNTERFLASHING

METAL COVER

SADDLE

CALK EDGES

BOARDS OR
PLYWOOD

FLASHING

SHINGLES

From: *Roofing and Siding*

TAKE NOTE

TAKE NOTE: Chimney saddle

If you have a chimney, don't be surprised to see an odd-looking, angled shape directly behind it, where it meets the downward slope of the roof. To protect that area from leaks due to trapped water and snow, roofers often install a cricket or saddle in addition to conventional flashing. Like a miniature pitched roof angled toward the back of the chimney, a saddle's center ridge creates two slopes that divert water around the sides of the chimney and mitigate the potential to trap water or snow at that joint.

Once the felt is attached (typically with staples, sometimes with short, fat nails), the roof penetrations and other critical areas must be flashed. As with windows (see Chapter 5), roof flashing protects areas that are the most vulnerable to water leakage, such as the valleys (where two roof slopes intersect, creating a gutter to the eave), and the various openings, such as vent pipes, chimneys and dormers. Roof leak problems in new homes almost always can be traced back to inadequate or poorly installed flashing.

Most flashing material is made of light-gauge, galvanized sheet metal or aluminum. On valleys, it is best installed in a continuous length to eliminate any joints that could allow water to penetrate to

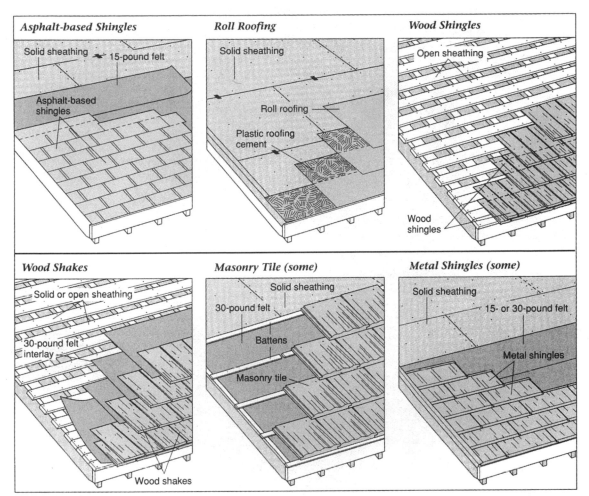

Asphalt-based Shingles
Solid sheathing — 15-pound felt
Asphalt-based shingles

Roll Roofing
Solid sheathing
Roll roofing
Plastic roofing cement

Wood Shingles
Open sheathing
Wood shingles

Wood Shakes
Solid or open sheathing
30-pound felt interlay
Wood shakes

Masonry Tile (some)
Solid sheathing
30-pound felt
Battens
Masonry tile

Metal Shingles (some)
Solid sheathing
15- or 30-pound felt
Metal shingles

From: *Roofing & Siding*

Roofing materials are not created (or installed) equally, with various sheathing, underlayment and fastening requirements.

the felt and roof sheathing; a crimp at the end mitigates the chance that runoff will splash up under the shingles. At protrusions, metal flashing is cut, fastened and sealed with a mastic to properly shed water away from the pipe, chimney or other projection.

Increasingly, vent pipes are sold with integral flashing, a skirt-like metal panel at the base that is secured to the roof.

For most roofs of conventional size and design, installation of felt and flashing takes about a day, perhaps into the next, before the roofers can begin applying the finish material.

Roofing paper and flashing

Approx. time (days): 1
Cum. time (days):....47-62

Roofing Materials and Installation

The most popular type of roofing for new-home construction is asphalt composition shingles, or simply "comp roofing" in builder lingo. It consists of a thin mat of fiber glass or tar-soaked felt with a top coating of mineral-based granules. The granules serve both a practical and aesthetic purpose: they protect the base from fire damage and the sun's ultraviolet rays, and are selected, arranged and bonded to the mat in various colors and patterns. Sometimes, they can be made to simulate tile or wood shakes. Often, the more expensive types have multiple mats and feature granules that are ingeniously arranged to give the impression of a shadow or depth. In those cases, they are called dimensional shingles.

Like almost all roofing products, asphalt comp shingles are specified by their weight per "square" (a roofing term meaning 100 square feet), which generally indicates the durability and general performance of the material. Typically, new homes are roofed with 240-pound fiber glass comp shingles with a performance warranty of about 20 to 25 years, the expected useful life span of the material. By contrast, some heavyweight shingles weighing up to 380 pounds per square have warranties of perhaps 40 years. Increasingly, fiber glass mats are replacing organic (tar and cellulose) mats because the synthetic material achieves a higher fire rating.

Comp roofing is commonly installed in what's called a three-tab profile, in which the shingle panel is separated into three sections by slender notches. In essence, this design allows a section of three shingles to be installed at once, saving time. The notches in a three-tab design help the roofers stagger the shingles for a more dimensional appearance and to avoid creating long channels for water runoff in the notches. Commonly, the shingles and notches align every other course, or layer, from the eaves to the ridge.

Starting from the eaves, the top portion of each shingle section is nailed to the

Asphalt or "comp" shingles can be made to replicate a variety of roof finishes, including cedar shakes and slate.

Photo: Rich Binsacca

126

Photo: Kevin Berne

roof deck (except in some high-wind areas, it isn't required that all roofing nails hit a rafter or other structural member). The bottom edge of the next course of shingles conceals the fasteners. At the ridge and along other peaks (where two upward roof slopes intersect, such as on a hip-style roof), roofers install cap shingles, which mould over the peaks or ridges to enclose the roof and shed water to either side.

The next most-popular roofing material for new homes is cedar shingles. Properly installed and ventilated from below (by open sheathing or other means), cedar shingles can last 50 years or more. Typically, because they are incorrectly installed over solid sheathing or without adequate air circulation to dry them out after a snow or rain storm, wood shingles last only about 25 years, perhaps less if exposed to extreme climates or shaded by overhanging trees. Untreated, cedar shingles also can be a fire hazard; as such, several local code jurisdictions require a fire coating or simply ban them from new homes and even re-roofing projects.

The main difference between comp roofing and wood shingles, besides materially, is that cedar is applied one shingle at a time. The

Asphalt or "comp" shingles are the most popular roofing finish, and are easily and quickly applied with air-driven staples.

Lingo:

hip-style roof—a roof design where all sides are angled toward the ridge, creating a pyramid-like appearance.

open sheathing—roof sheathing applied or attached in long, thin strips (as opposed to full panels or sheets of plywood) with gaps between the strips to facilitate air flow from the attic to the roof finish.

Roofing installation
Approx. time (days): 2
Cum. time (days):....49-64

installer not only has to only pay more attention to maintaining a straight line along each course, but to creating and properly staggering the joints between the shingles to allow for moisture expansion of wet shingles.

While asphalt comp and cedar shingles dominate the market, architectural styles, regional preferences and a return to historic and nostalgic architecture in new-home construction has fostered demand for other roofing materials. Clay and concrete tiles, stone shingles, metal panels and even plastic shingles (moulded to look like a natural material, such as cedar) are available in various types, sizes, styles and colors, with both design and functional value.

For obvious geographic, architectural and cultural reasons, clay, concrete and ceramic tile roofing is most often seen on roofs in the Gulf and desert states, or on any new homes built in the Mediterranean style. By contrast, slate roofing is commonly seen on Colonial or Early American-style homes, though most new, mass-market houses in these styles actually have asphalt comp roofing designed to replicate their stone predecessors.

With any cementitious or true stone material, the roof structure must be engineered to handle the extra weight, perhaps up to 600 pounds per square. The material also must be properly fastened (with nails, through the sheathing), especially in high-wind areas where failure or tear-off creates dangerous projectiles. To address both concerns, roofing manufacturers offer lightweight, polymer-reinforced products with pre-drilled nail holes.

Like tile and stone, metal roofing has a place in new-home construction. However, it is more expensive than either asphalt comp or cedar shingles to purchase and install, and thus is often only put on tract homes located in heavy snow areas or, more commonly, by special request from the homeowner.

Plastic roofing, an infant in the market, is often sold in large, 4x8 panels that replicate a staggered shingle pattern to speed installation. Because of the material composition, the panels also are lightweight and easy to handle.

On conventional tract homes, it takes perhaps two days to apply the roofing finish, longer if there are several peaks and valleys, odd angles or steep pitches to deal with.

Photo: Kevin Berne

Vinyl siding applies in long sections that are easily cut to fit around windows and at corners.

Siding

A home's siding serves several purposes. It is, in fact, the primary decorative feature of the house, establishing or reinforcing its architectural style. Siding also is a backdrop or canvas for trim, lighting and landscaping. Finally, it protects the house from the elements.

The variety of exterior siding products for new homes is extensive, including traditional brick, stucco and horizontal clapboards. In new housing, it is common to see these and other materials in combination, such as a stone ledge accenting stucco, or a brick facade with clapboard siding on the side and rear elevations.

Siding and trim installation
Approx. time (days):.....2-4
Cum. time (days):....51-68

Such combinations provide visual interest and diversity among what is often a homogeneous architectural style throughout the homes in a subdivision. Doing so also saves money without losing much perceived value. A brick facade, for instance, is impressive, but less costly than applying brick on sides of the house that people rarely see. Similarly, a stone or brick accent adds substance and mass to a lighter (and less expensive) finish material, such as stucco or clapboard siding.

It would be a waste of good paper to run down the list of exterior siding materials and how they are applied. Rather, as a new home-owner watching workers install whatever material you or your builder selected, you should be aware of a few things.

Wood Siding

Clapboard, or horizontal, siding is a staple of American housing architecture, especially as new-home designs meld the details of several styles. Once almost exclusively solid wood (such as redwood or cedar), synthetic siding materials are more often the norm on new homes. Vinyl and (to a decreasing extent) aluminum are common on more affordable homes, while composite wood and lightweight cementitious panels are often used on higher-priced houses.

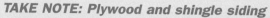

TAKE NOTE: Plywood and shingle siding

To a lesser extent on new production or tract housing, and often because of market or installation considerations, builders may use plywood siding or cedar shingles to finish the exterior walls.

Plywood siding is similar to another layer of sheathing, except that the exterior or exposed face of the panels are moulded with a pattern often simulating vertical or horizontal clapboards. The key advantage of plywood siding is that it applies faster than individual wood or composite clapboard finishes, and is far cheaper than "true" wood siding, making it attractive for affordable housing projects.

Cedar shingle siding sits at the opposite end of the spectrum. While relatively inexpensive as a product, the volume of cedar shingles required to finish an entire house is often cost prohibitive. The expense of properly and carefully applying the shingles is out of reach for most middle-market or price-sensitive housing developments. In addition, cedar shingle siding is an architectural statement. It is best applied to Queen Anne, Craftsman or vacation homes, which are less common in production home construction.

To make cedar shingles more affordable, some manufacturers pre-apply them in various patterns onto plywood panels, which attach to the exterior walls more quickly than installing individual shingles. The shingles are arranged to overlap and conceal the substrate and fasteners. For the most part, builders use these shingled panels to accent or add dimension to a facade.

Because clapboard siding (and any exterior finish) is so exposed to the outside elements, builders and siding subs must make provisions to allow for expansion and contraction of the material when the cli-

Photo: Rich Binsacca

The trick to lap siding, whether wood or vinyl, is to limit the number of joints and create a smooth surface along the length of the elevation.

mate changes. Vinyl siding, for instance, is installed "loose," that is, the clapboards aren't held tight to the side of the house, but rather hang loosely (if securely) from the exterior walls.

Doing so allows air circulation behind the siding to dry out any moisture that penetrates the surface (such as during a wind-driven rain) and also accommodates expansion and contraction of the material in extreme weather conditions. If held tight to the house, vinyl siding might buckle or show a wavy surface as it expands or contracts without the room to do so.

Similarly, wood, wood composites and cementitious clapboard siding materials must be allowed to "breathe" and accommodate the elements. Though they are held tight to the exterior walls (as there is less chance of moisture getting through), a small gap is left between adjoining or abutting panels to allow expansion along the length of the panels, the direction most wood-based siding products swell. Occasionally, abutting panels are mitered (or angled) to each other to better conceal the joint. One note: the gaps, or joints, between panels on wood or synthetic siding should be staggered to avoid creating water channels.

TAKE NOTE

TAKE NOTE: Hardboard siding

In recent years, the performance of hardboard siding, a wood-composite clapboard product, has come under fire for various moisture-related problems, including swelling, distortion, de-lamination and mold growth. Most of the cases occurred on new homes built in areas of high humidity or rainfall, such as the Gulf coast and Pacific Northwest, where the siding has less opportunity to dry out from wind-driven rain and high levels of airborne moisture.

While an affordable and generally reliable product, hardboard siding should be avoided in such geographic areas or climatic conditions. If your builder uses it, ask him or her about the recent problems associated with the product and how it is being addressed. Common solutions include factory priming of all surfaces (and perhaps even pre-painted panels), the use of a vapor retarder on exterior walls or furring them out to create a small airspace behind the siding, and even inserting weep holes at the bottom edges, thus allowing hardboard siding to dry out or drain moisture build-up.

Lingo:

primed—a product that is covered by a protective layer before finishing, such as with paint.

furring out—the use of non-structural wood or metal framing components attached to concrete or masonry walls for the fastening of drywall or other wall substrate or finish; in essence, a false wall or nailing surface.

Shingle siding offers a distinctive look, but can be expensive to install and maintain.

In addition, most wood composite and cementitious clapboard products are primed on all surfaces at the factory, mitigating most water or moisture damage to the surface or between the siding and the exterior wall sheathing. The surface of the panels (or "exposure") is then finished on site, typically with an industrial paint sprayer.

Photo: Rich Binsacca

Veneer brick siding or accents still require the special skills and tools of a mason.

Photo: Rich Binsacca

Brick Siding

Another popular exterior finish is brick. Very few new homes these days are constructed with brick as a structural material, but brick veneer remains a staple of new-home construction as an exterior finish material. Whether applied as full-size or as a thin veneer (half-brick) over the exterior walls, brick gives the perception of a solid house and of lasting, durable value.

Full brick veneer requires that the foundation wall has a ledge to support the brick. The mason begins here to lay the brick. Every other course or so, as the brick wall climbs vertically, the mason will connect the brick wall with metal ties, which are nailed to the framed wall and set in the brick's mortar. Because bricks and the mortar between them are porous, the system is subject to moisture and water infiltration, which can eventually damage the exterior walls and even the structure if left unchecked. A common method for helping dry out the wall is to leave a finger space, a thin gap (about the thickness of your index finger) between the brick veneer and the exterior walls.

Lingo:

weep holes—gaps left in masonry (brick, concrete block or stucco) to drain water and moisture trapped behind it.

Stucco siding is a popular masonry finish, especially on Mediterranean and French Colonial-style homes.

Near or at the bottom course of bricks, the mason also will leave gaps in the mortar to allow water to drain out from behind the veneer wall. These weep holes do not affect the structural value of the veneer. In fact, without them, the system is more likely to fail.

Among exterior finishes, brick is popular for its superior durability and long-term good looks. It never goes out of style, makes a house

Photo: United States Gypsum

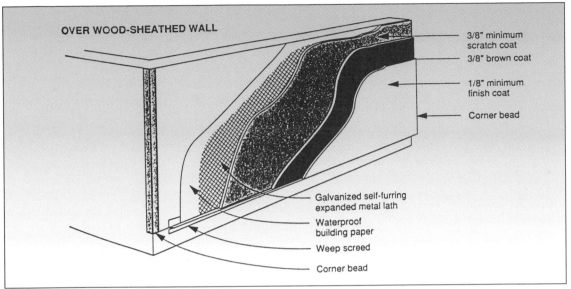

OVER WOOD-SHEATHED WALL

3/8" minimum scratch coat

3/8" brown coat

1/8" minimum finish coat

Corner bead

Galvanized self-furring expanded metal lath

Waterproof building paper

Weep screed

Corner bead

From: *How to Build a Wood-Framed House*

appear more solid and well-built and, as a result, often commands a premium price as an optional upgrade or as the signature feature of a house.

The main complaint against brick is its cost. Full bricks are among the most expensive exterior finish materials, and masonry is a highly skilled (and paid) trade. That's why many new production or tract homes feature brick as an accent material on the exterior, or applied only to one elevation (typically the front).

Stucco Siding

Stucco is another, typically less expensive, masonry finish material. Used extensively on commercial and other non-residential buildings because of its durability and relative ease of application, stucco has found its way onto several different housing styles, from Mediterranean to Tudor, Craftsman and ranch styles. In the melting pot of today's new-home exterior facades, stucco has become common.

Both true and synthetic (or insulated) stucco is applied in stages, albeit with slight differences. True stucco begins with a galvanized wire mesh or lath (often chicken wire) attached with staples or "U"-shaped nails to completely cover the exterior walls or wherever the stucco will be applied. Held slightly away from the wall, the wire serves to hold the initial layer of plaster in place as it dries, creating a solid surface for one or two subsequent layers to come.

Lingo:

lath—a thin strip of wood or series of strips attached to a wall.

135

The initial coating of thick, grainy plaster applied to the mesh is called the scratch coat. Applied in much the same way as drywall joint compound (see Chapter 5) and to a thickness of about ⅜-inch, it is the most textured layer, completely masking the wire. It sufficiently dries within a day or so, creating a rough surface that better adheres to the next layer, called the brown coat.

Though just as thick as the previous layer, the brown coat is applied more smoothly than the scratch coat, evening out indentations or other glitches in the scratch coat toward a smooth exterior finish. It also dries within a day, at which time the finish coat is applied.

Textured or smoothed out with a trowel, the finish coat is only about ⅛-inch thick. Occasionally, to avoid having to paint the finish coat, masons or stucco installers will mix in a dye as they prepare the finish coat, creating a color that carries through the material.

Though stucco is somewhat porous, and certainly wet when applied, it's rare to see structural problems or critical moisture or water damage. If so, they occur primarily through framed openings (windows) or near the foundation. Where there is damage, it is mostly cosmetic, shown as water stains or small cracks, especially at corners and joints. In a slab-on-grade foundation, the installer may groove a few control joints in long expanses of stucco to direct and better conceal shrinkage cracks.

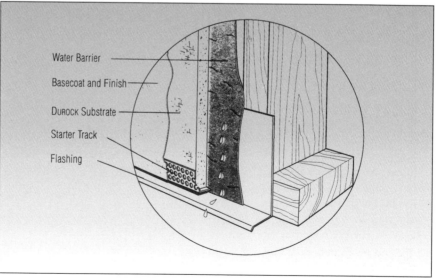

EIFS, or "synthetic" stucco, applies faster than true stucco and features an insulating layer between the finish and the framed wall. Flashing at windows and edges is particularly critical with EIFS.

United States Gypsum

EIFS

In the past 15 years or so, synthetic stucco, also known as an Exterior Insulated Finishing System (EIFS), has made inroads into both commercial and residential construction, replacing (and presumably improving on) true stucco.

Like true stucco, EIFS is applied in layers. The first membrane consists of thin, rigid foam panels, applied much like drywall or plywood, which serve as the insulating layer. Next, a fiber mesh is applied to serve as the lath, much like the wire mesh used with true stucco.

With EIFS, the scratch and brown coats are often the same layer, though still just ⅜-inch thick. Mixed with polymers and other bonding agents, this combined layer is more durable—and certainly less time-consuming to apply—than conventional stucco applications.

The finish coat, mixed with plasticizers for added durability and flexibility under extreme conditions or climate changes, is applied and textured similar to real stucco, leaving an exterior finish virtually undetectable from the true thing.

EIFS, however, has received some bad press recently from reports of failures and significant structural water damage from moisture trapped behind the stucco facade, primarily from poorly flashed (or even unflashed) windows. Cases of rotted wall sheathing and even structural framing components have led to EIFS bans by homeowners' associations and local code jurisdictions.

Unlike the problems with hardboard siding, there seems to be no geographic or climatic consistency with EIFS failures. Rather, the problems appear to be borne of inadequate product design and poor installation.

TAKE NOTE: The first course

Regardless of the exterior siding used, the bottom edge or starter course of the material should be held at least six inches above the finished grade of the lot. In many areas this is dictated by code. Though doing so exposes the unfinished concrete of the foundation or exterior wall sheathing, it mitigates the chance for ground-level moisture to find its way up to and behind the exterior finishes, where it can damage the sheathing and even the structural framing, and also cause stains and other distortions on both exterior and interior surfaces.

Photo: Rich Binsacca

Using several siding materials — in this case stucco, lap siding, and a stone accent — lowers the cost of any one material and adds a distinctive touch to new homes.

To compensate, EIFS manufacturers may offer insulation panels with slight grooves on the outside face, designed to shed water and condensation that infiltrate the system. Better still, builders and EIFS installers should make sure that windows and other framed openings in the walls are properly flashed and that the fiber mesh and subsequent layers of stucco wrap the underside of the insulation panels near the foundation, where ground moisture can "wick up" under the system.

Stone Siding

Lingo:

wick up—the migration of moisture from one area to another.

In some markets, the use of stone is making a comeback, chiefly as an exterior trim or accent for an otherwise clapboard or stucco finish. Like stucco, stone is available as the real thing or as a synthetic veneer replica. As the makers of replica stone improve the randomization of their rock designs, textures, colors and layouts, builders and homeowners will be more apt to swap out real stone, which is often more expensive and difficult to apply. Real or faux, stone work is time consuming; even a small job can take a few days or more in order to properly arrange and secure the stones in place.

Trim and Lighting

If part of the exterior design scheme, the application of trim and lighting finishes the outside of the structure. At a minimum, builders will add casing around windows and doors to show a more finished appearance, and put porch lights by all exterior doors.

Trim elements include dentil mouldings, fascia, shutters and soffits, helping enclose and finish the exterior.

Photo: Rich Binsacca

The base of any down-spout and gutter system should have a splash block or gravel bed that dissipates or carries water away from the house and foundation.

Lingo:

casing—the trim work or moulding around a door or window.

fascia—a length of wood or other material attached to the ends of the roof rafters or joists to enclose them, similar to the perimeter beam attached to the floor joists.

soffit—the underside of the rafters, often enclosed to protect the roof structure from moisture or other infiltration and hazards.

rake—the overhang of a roof over a gable end.

For more expensive spec homes, the builder may add false shutters on the windows, thicker door and window casings, a detailed fascia, soffit or rake (which enclose overhanging rafters or roof sections) and perhaps carved columns, porch railings or other features. Lighting might extend to a few sentries on either side of the garage door, a lamp post at the head of a pathway and a more extensive package to illuminate the front door.

Occasionally, the exterior finish material is used as a trim feature, as well. Using rigid foam panels cut into desired shapes and angles, stucco installers can create ornamental cornices or bump-outs that appear to be thicker sections of the wall, typically along the lower third of the structure. The same effect can be accomplished with an additional layer of brick veneer. Non-structural, these tricks serve to boost the massing of the house for a more solid appearance or feel.

By contrast, contemporary homes and those of a strict Mediterranean or pueblo style are often finished without trim, but instead completed in just a single material, such as stucco. These homes, however, are rare in production or speculative housing, as builders are more apt to provide homes with mass-market appeal and more traditional finishes and details.

Gutters

Once the roofing and siding are applied and finished, the gutter system is installed. Gutters, downspouts and accessories to the system, made of metal or plastic in various colors, profiles and sizes, are essential to protect the house from water damage, especially at the foundation. Clogged or improperly installed gutters (the horizontal run) and downspouts (the vertical pipes) can cause stains on the siding and trim, foster mold and mildew on the shingles and allow water to collect at the base of the house, perhaps causing hydrostatic pressure on (and eventually leaks through) the foundation.

The placement of the downspouts determines the length, location and slope of the gutters that feed them. Typically, downspouts are placed at the corners of the house, generally out of sight and to direct water away from the house. Occasionally, if valleys are created by the roof design, a downspout might have to be placed near the front door or some other more noticeable place.

Once the location of the downspouts is determined (if not installed), the gutters go in. There are several ways to attach gutters, sometimes even before the roofing goes on, but the common method is with a series of long nails through rigid metal conduits from the front of the gutter to the fascia, a continuous board attached to the ends of the rafters (or rafter tails). Lacking a fascia board, the gutters are attached to the ends of the rafters or hung from the eaves.

Gutters are installed with a slight slope toward the nearest downspout to direct water runoff from the roof. The slope should be almost imperceptible from the curb, perhaps an inch difference along a ten-foot length of gutter.

At the base of the downspouts, depending on the slope of the finished grade or lot, the builder may install extenders—hinged sections of pipe that extend the downspout mouth farther from the house and foundation. Or, the end of the downspout may simply have a splash block, a wedge-shaped piece of cast concrete or rigid plastic that disperses runoff from the downspout and gutters above. Splash blocks may also be simply a bed of washed gravel at the base of a downspout.

Lingo:

massing—the overall proportion of a house and its features to the structure and the surrounding elements or lot.

hydrostatic pressure—pressure exerted by water on a structure, commonly the foundation.

Swales or catch basins collect runoff from several homes in a subdivision.

Photo: Rich Binsacca

Drainage, Fences and Other Features

In large residential developments, builders are often required to provide drainage away from the homes to the street, swale or other collection area nearby. Often designed and excavated during the early stages of construction (during lot or neighborhood grading), swales and other drainage conditions carry water runoff from several homes to the sewer system.

Commonly, lots are graded to passively direct water runoff from rain, snow and even landscape irrigation to a swale or other collection area. But when lots are stepped on a hillside, for instance, the builder will also install a sloping, concrete ditch (or V-ditch) between properties to catch and carry water to the street or swale so that it does not flow into an adjacent lot.

Similarly, hillside lots often require structural retaining walls to keep loose dirt and mud from sliding into a neighboring property and causing damage to the house or other features. Retaining walls are commonly built out of reinforced poured concrete, concrete blocks (with each course reinforced with rebar and stepped back up the hill for extra leverage) or sections of wood, such as railroad ties, laid horizontally between steel beams.

Lingo:

swale—a gently sloped trough behind or in close proximity to a house or houses that captures and carries drainage from rain, snow and other sources away from the property.

142

A concrete V-ditch (so called because of its shape) collects and carries water away from hillside or sloping home sites to the street or a catch basin.

Photo: Rich Binsacca

Interlocking concrete pavers or bricks are a stylish alternative to paved pathways and other hardscape features.

Depending on local requirements or site conditions, the building department may require the builder or developer to construct retaining walls as part of the basic infrastructure of the neighborhood (streets, sidewalks, curbs and gutters) to avoid any slides or other hazards during excavation and construction.

Walkways to the front door and backyard concrete patios are often part of the builder's

Photo: Interlocking Concrete Paver Institute

143

A finished deck is a popular add-on to most new homes, though builders rarely install them as part of their normal scope of work.

Photo: Trex Company LLC

Like a slab foundation, the front pathway is typically formed and poured with concrete.

Photo: Rich Binsacca

exterior finish work. Created in the same fashion as a slab foundation, these areas are typically formed to a four-inch depth, reinforced with a medium-gauge metal mesh or grid and poured either from a concrete truck and boom (see Chapter 2) or with concrete mixed on the job site. Commonly, the foundation contractor is

Finished tract homes often feature a variety of exterior finishes, such as lap siding with brick accents, to add visual interest and increase value.

Photo: Rich Binsacca

brought back to do the job, applying his finishing skills to achieve the proper mix, smooth out the surfaces and groove control joints.

Unlike patios, putting up a fence on your property is most commonly left up to you, the homeowner, after move-in. However, you may be able to contract the construction of a perimeter or privacy fence with your builder before his or her job is done.

The same holds true for decks and landscaping (beyond, perhaps, the installation of sod in the front yard), as most home builders have neither the time, interest, or particular skill to do either job. Better to hire a deck builder or framing carpenter for any backyard additions and a landscaper or landscape architect for the plantings. ∎

CHAPTER

Interior Finishes

Photo: Weather Shield Windows & Doors

Window trim is just one of several interior finishes that must be applied before a home is completed.

The next time you walk by your kitchen, stop and take a mental inventory of the various products and systems it contains. Appliances (obviously), a sink and faucet, cabinets—that's the basic list. Then there's the flooring, lighting, ventilation (for the range or cook top) and vent registers, countertops, paint and/or wallpaper and perhaps ceramic tile along the back of the work surfaces, doors to other rooms and a window, cased in a decorative trim, to capture a view and bring in light.

The kitchen, in fact, embodies the scope of finishes that are typically applied inside a new home. It's a long list of often small items and many finishes that requires special contractors or installers working either in close proximity or, more commonly, in sequence. To be sure, the kitchen is an anomaly; few other rooms in the house, except perhaps the bathrooms, contain so many different products and systems. Still, it's indicative of the coordination, time and extent of work required to finish a home for occupancy.

As with exterior finishes, it would be difficult to list all the possible options and explain their application and individual pros and cons. In fact, builders prefer the narrowest possible range in order to do the job quickly and for the least cost. Unless pushed by some marketing edict or the particular selection of a home buyer, they'll generally apply very bland (some say "classic" or "traditional") finishes on the inside.

Even in the kitchens and baths, the rooms that draw the most attention, builders are careful not to exclude any potential home buyer by taking a risk with wild finishes. Those that showcase odd-colored cabinets, a dramatic countertop material or a deviant tile pattern or finish often do so in the context of a model home, to display the range and possibilities of pricier options and to create memory points in the shoppers' minds. In the homes built on speculation, hoping to attract the broadest range of home buyers, a builder finds his budget often results in a more conservative approach.

Within those parameters, though, successful builders pick their spots to attract attention from buyers. Oak flooring, while not flashy, is very desirable and classy; solid-surface countertops with a contrasting border appear more expensive without much of a premium cost. Thick baseboard trim and crown mouldings, when appropriate to the style of the house, add a sense of depth, dimension and added value.

Basic or not, interior finishes take time. First, the overall process is a collection of little tasks, such as attaching electrical faceplates, vent registers and towel racks. In addition, the various contractors and installers must be coordinated depending on their availability and in a logical sequence, a schedule that is rarely smooth or without some delay or downtime between crews of workers.

Lingo:

model home—one or more homes built to showcase the floor plans and finishes offered by a builder in a speculative housing development, allowing prospective home buyers to tour finished and decorated homes before purchasing.

crown mouldings—an ornamental or decorative piece attached at the junction of the interior walls and ceiling.

Finally, finish work is more meticulous and slow compared to rough framing and mechanicals. Unlike a wall stud or duct run, the work will be on display. Any flaw is exaggerated, every gap or missing piece highlighted. For these reasons, the application of interior finishes takes more time to complete. The upside is that, once it's over, you can move in. The downside is that you feel like you've waited long enough already, and the house is so close to being done now that your patience is on a razor's edge.

Remarkably, however, some home buyers who visit their new house within a few weeks of a promised or scheduled delivery date are amazed at how much may still need to be done. With the carpeting yet to be installed, loose wires awaiting fixtures and appliances still boxed up in the garage, new buyers often think there's no way their home will be done in time.

In fact, the installation of appliances and lighting fixtures and the application of carpeting are among the least time-consuming tasks of finishing a house. In addition, those items often are installed near the end of the job to avoid intruding on any lingering finish work or being damaged by subcontractors and their materials.

Wall Finishes

In new production housing, the wall finishes generally consist of paint and wallpaper. Ceramic tile (beyond the bathroom or perhaps the kitchen), veneer stone, wood paneling or other wall finishes or texturing are either offered as optional upgrades or special orders on most production homes.

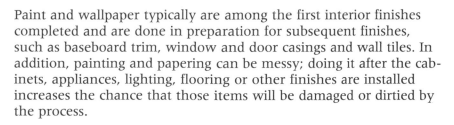

TAKE NOTE: *Touch-ups*

Because painting is often the first interior finish applied, it can get chipped and scraped as succeeding finishes are applied by the traffic of work crews and materials. In fact, you may see such damage as you conduct a formal walk-through with your builder upon completion of the home (see Chapter 8). Before you move in, however, the builder will call the paint contractor back to "touch up" the walls and trim, bringing the entire interior finishing stage full circle.

Paint and wallpaper typically are among the first interior finishes completed and are done in preparation for subsequent finishes, such as baseboard trim, window and door casings and wall tiles. In addition, painting and papering can be messy; doing it after the cabinets, appliances, lighting, flooring or other finishes are installed increases the chance that those items will be damaged or dirtied by the process.

Lingo:

optional upgrades— items, finishes or products available to a home buyer at extra cost.

TAKE NOTE: Mouldings

Most wood trim work, especially crown mouldings, is built up; that is, separate components (or profiles) are used to create what eventually appears to be a singular profile or pattern. On a crown mould, for instance, a flat piece of wood, such as a 1x4, is held tight to the wall-ceiling joint to provide a nailing base. Subsequent profiles, angled from the bottom edge of the base piece to the ceiling (leaving a hollow area behind them) are built or layered on each other until the desired profile is achieved. Finish nails (those with small heads) are countersunk into the trim, puttied over, sanded and finished to conceal them from view.

To help reduce the cost of hiring a finish carpenter to craft a crown or baseboard profile, many production builders turn to pre-moulded trim. Made from a rigid foam, the trim sections are moulded into a variety of profiles and primed at the factory, ready for paint. In fact, in the factory, manufacturers can create traditional, Old-World details that, if done on site, would require the professional skills of a plasterer or woodworker.

Moulded trim can be cut with standard tools and installed either with nails or high-strength adhesive. Once finished, pre-moulded trim is virtually indistinguishable from a built-up wood or plaster profile.

Paint (walls)
Approx. time (days): 2
Cum. time (days):....53-70

Lingo:

door thresholds—a strip of moulded material placed on the floor between the jamb of a door to seal the door, facilitate a transition or change in floor finishes between rooms and/or provide weather protection.

mitered—a beveled or angled cut, usually at 45 degrees, at the end of a piece of wood or lumber.

trim profile—the shape, design and details of the trim or moulding.

countersunk—screwing or nailing the head of a fastener below the surface of the wood to conceal or protect it.

Paint

There's really no trick to interior painting, except that yet another subcontractor must be scheduled and coordinated among all the others trying to finish the house. Unencumbered by other finishes, the painter's job is done primarily with a sprayer (for walls), usually at least two coats thick (thus requiring two days to complete).

Trim

Once the paint has sufficiently dried, finish carpenters enter the scene to fasten the various trim components, including baseboard, crown mouldings, door thresholds and casings around the doors, windows and passage openings. Trim work is (or should be) meticulous. Adjoining sections of trim should be mitered (or cut at an angle, rather than square-cut), masked by putty and sanded to create a seamless appearance.

Most trim is made of wood, often pine or oak, and installed unfinished. Occasionally, the trim can be ordered with a finish, such as a stain or varnish, or primed for paint. However, the installation process, including joint connections and nail holes, requires the trim to be puttied, sanded and refinished regardless. Some contemporary or affordable homes eschew trim work entirely, leaving the painted walls blank, thus eliminating the time and expense of a trim or finish carpenter and materials while achieving a sleek look.

Trim Paint

Once the trim is installed, the painter returns to prime and paint it, or perhaps apply a stain or varnish to finish the job. The painter masks his previous work with tape or paper on the walls to protect it from getting splattered by the trim finish. But the process, done with a brush instead of a sprayer or roller, is time consuming and

Trim (installation and finish
Approx. time (days): 1
Cum. time (days):....13-15

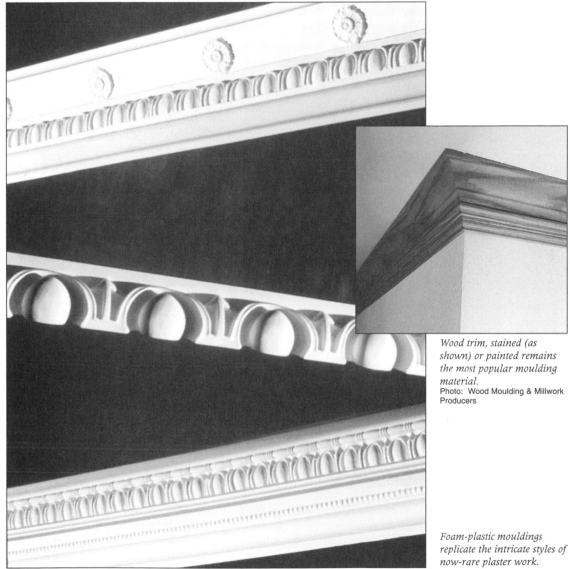

Photo: Style-Mark

Wood trim, stained (as shown) or painted remains the most popular moulding material.
Photo: Wood Moulding & Millwork Producers

Foam-plastic mouldings replicate the intricate styles of now-rare plaster work.

often requires at least two coats of paint in addition to a primer coat. Unlike the walls, painting the trim can require a few days to perhaps a week, depending on the painter's schedule and the size and scope of the trim work inside.

Wallpaper

Like painting, wallpapering is a fairly simple procedure, though it too often calls for the services of an expert installer. As such, wallpaper is most commonly offered to new-home buyers as an optional upgrade item for the kitchen, bathrooms, bedrooms or perhaps a home office or library.

As with wild paint colors or exterior finishes, builders are careful not to take fashion risks with wallpaper because it is often a very personal choice driven by particular tastes and trends. While a production builder may use it to dress up or highlight a model home, rarely will it be hung in a spec home unless the buyer requests (and pays extra) for it.

**Flooring
(carpet not included)**
Approx. time (days): 2
Cum. time (days):....59-76

Flooring

Except for carpeting, the various flooring materials in a house are often the next finishes applied after the walls and trim are completed. Simply, vinyl, ceramic tile and hardwood flooring installs faster and easier when it doesn't have to be cut around cabinets, appliances or plumbing fixtures. Once the floor finishes are installed (or "down"), the subcontractor or site superintendent will typically cover them with a thick sheet of plastic or kraft paper, especially along high-traffic areas, to mitigate damage during the rest of the interior finish work.

Vinyl

There's very little mystery to flooring installation. Vinyl flooring, either cut from rolled sheets or put down in a pattern of one-foot-square tiles, is applied over a mastic—an exceptionally strong adhesive. If using a sheet product, the installer typically cuts it to the general shape of the room, such as the kitchen or bathroom. He then applies the mastic to a small section of the floor (cleaned of dust and dirt, and leveled, if necessary), carefully pressing the vinyl from a given edge and making more precise cuts as he goes to ensure a tight fit to the edges of the room.

While it would be possible to precisely cut the sheet to the dimensions of the floor, the material is stiff and difficult to handle in large sections from its rolled condition. Installers strive for as few joints as possible, so cutting the roll into smaller sections is often frowned

Photo: Congoleum

Sheet vinyl (or resilient) flooring is an increasingly popular material for kitchens and baths, combining style and low maintenance.

upon, if not specifically prohibited by the builder unless absolutely necessary given the size or shape of the room. Ideally, the floor of a room should be covered in one sheet, with no joints.

The mastic, in fact, helps secure a manageable portion of the vinyl sheet to the subfloor, allowing the installer to make the final cuts to

Photo: Crossville Ceramics

Ceramic tile can be used for floors, walls and countertops, providing a classic look, highlighted by accent tiles and premoulded patterns.

Lingo:

mortar—a mixture of concrete paste and aggregate (rock or minerals) used to connect or secure ceramic or stone tiles to a surface.

fit the room. The glue dries quickly, so, if spread around the entire floor all at once, it would develop a thin skin that would render its adhesive value useless before the flooring, whether from a sheet or tiles, could be applied on top of it.

Like sheet vinyl flooring, vinyl tiles (as well as ceramic or stone flooring tiles in a foyer or elsewhere) are applied in smaller sections, either over mastic or, for the ceramics and stone products, cement mortar. The installer will lay out perhaps a dozen tiles at a time, often starting at a corner. If it appears that some tiles will have to be cut, the installer may begin near the center so that cut tiles will be placed along the edges of the room or eventually hidden under appliances or cabinets. This layout process also allows the installer to make cuts precisely, working to form tiles around door openings, angled walls or other intrusions as he goes.

On occasion, especially in custom or contract homes (as opposed to spec or tract homes), the precise layout of the tiles may have been determined and drawn by a designer, showing the location of full tiles and cut tiles, if necessary. The installer, therefore, simply follows the plan.

Just as sheet products are applied progressively, so are vinyl and ceramic tiles—so that the small patch of mastic or mortar remains fresh enough to properly adhere the products to the subfloor. Depending on the size and number of rooms requiring vinyl or ceramic tile flooring, complete installation of all flooring applications may take a few days.

Wood
Like vinyl and ceramic or stone flooring, wood flooring is also applied around this time. Gaining popularity in more places than just the foyer, these long, thin planks can be found in the kitchen, living and dining rooms, providing a classic, easy-to-maintain finish.

Once covered by carpeting in homes built during the first half of the 20th century, floors are now often covered in hardwood, which many consider a statement of added value and expense, something to be showcased and admired. As wood resources diminish, however, the cost of wood flooring has increased, creating a dilemma between a builder's budget and marketing savvy.

Hardwood flooring manufacturers have been able to keep costs somewhat in check with more efficient production practices and by using oak, maple and other species as veneers over lesser-grade wood substrates. They also do a better job of sealing and protecting the planks with tough varnishes and other coatings, reducing on-site finishing and maintenance costs to the builder and, ultimately, the homeowner.

Like other flooring options, wood planks are applied in stages, usually over an adhesive or mastic. Most are formed with a tongue-and-groove design along their side edges, allowing them to fit snugly and securely to adjacent planks. They also may be nailed to the

A finished wood floor is a dramatic feature, especially in modern or contemporary homes. Photo: Kevin Berne

Installing wood plank flooring requires a careful layout to limit the number of cut or ripped pieces.
Photo: Kevin Berne

subfloor either through pre-drilled holes in the surface or concealed between the planks.

With its narrow profile, hardwood flooring is rarely cut (or ripped) along its long edge or length of a plank. If an installer has to make a rip cut, that plank is typically set along an outside edge, hugging a wall, with most of the exposed surface of the plank (and certainly the cut edge) concealed by baseboard or other trim, such as a door threshold.

Though planks are currently the most popular wood flooring, parquet or patterned wood flooring also is available and occasionally used in the foyer or other formal areas of the house. Parquet flooring appears to be an intricate, woven pattern of wood, but in fact is usually installed in large (12x12-inch) tiles that align the pattern.

They are installed similarly to ceramic or vinyl tile, with a mastic over the wood subfloor.

To most production builders, parquet flooring (like wood paneling) is often too anesthetically risky for its cost and is more difficult to maintain than plank wood flooring.

Carpet

Carpet
Approx. time (days): 2
Cum. time (days):....61-78

Among floor finishes, carpeting is the oddball, at least in the fact that it is often the last finish product installed before move-in rather than one of the first. Carpeting is also the most popular flooring choice in new homes, covering most living spaces and the bedrooms. Therefore, for those home buyers touring a nearly completed home, the extent of the unfinished (uncarpeted) subflooring makes it appear that the house is further from completion than perhaps it actually is.

When the time comes, carpet installation is a layered process. First, a pad or cushion is cut and laid over the area, though often not precisely or in a continuous piece because it will be concealed under the actual carpeting. Next, the carpet installer will apply tack strips along the perimeter of the room or area to be carpeted. These long, thin wood strips, nailed into the subfloor, feature angled spikes that will grab the edges of the carpet and allow the installer to stretch it to the other edges for a smooth, wrinkle-free application.

With the pad and tack strips down, the installer begins the process of rolling out and cutting the carpet to fit the edges or shape of the room. With an idea of both the dimensions of the room and the carpet, he or she will start at a point that will minimize, if not eliminate, the need for joints connecting two sections of carpet. In fact, the installer will often strive to end a section of carpet at a door opening or the start of another room (and perhaps a different floor finish), where a threshold or other transition can conceal a joint.

TAKE NOTE: Carpet pads

Unlike other flooring products, carpeting is rarely installed with an adhesive unless it can be put down in a smooth, even layer and kept from eking out through the carpet backing before it dries. Because cured (or dried) mastic leaves a hard surface, carpeting is best installed over a pad and a wood subfloor, allowing it to have a soft, giving texture and feel.

Even the smallest kitchen can benefit from the side-by-side utility cabinets which are much more flexible than a regular pantry.

Photo: Aristokraft, Inc.

Because carpet often is installed in several rooms and mostly covers large expanses, such as a living room or great room, and also involves a number of steps, it may take a few days before it is all in. To protect it, especially if the completed house is being sold on speculation and home shoppers are expected to tour the home, builders often will lay wide strips of plastic or kraft paper on top of the carpet to shepherd traffic through the house, then remove the protection before move-in.

Cabinets

Installed primarily in the kitchen and, to a lesser extent the bathrooms, cabinetry is logically the next phase of interior finishes because it provides the framework for countertops, appliances and perhaps lighting and other accessory products.

Cabinet Styles and Features

Cabinets are divided into two basic categories, wall and base, the latter of which rest on the floor. Every cabinet includes a box (the depth, width and height of the storage area) and fronts (the doors and drawers that "front" and enclose the boxes).

Within those basic parameters, though, exists a remarkable variety of choices, features and accessories that combine convenience and style. For instance, the boxes and fronts can be a European style, with concealed hinges, flat (or flush) fronts and no pulls or handles for very sleek, clean look. More traditional styles, commonly oak or maple with a raised-wood design on the fronts, feature exposed hinges and pulls for a more dimensional look. Within both styles

Cabinets these days are usually pre-manufactured boxes, which allow faster installation.

Photo: Kevin Berne

may be open shelving and glass-front cabinets that allow you to display (or simply see) certain items in the kitchen or provide some visual relief along a long run of wall cabinets.

There's also a lot going on inside the boxes. Aware of the trend toward more convenience and accessibility in the kitchen, cabinet makers now offer roll-out shelves, pull-out bread boards, spice racks, recycling bin holders, Lazy Susans and other accessories. Most also feature adjustable shelves to allow you to customize the storage inside the cabinets.

The dimension and shape of cabinets also has evolved, mostly in response to the tendency toward larger, more open kitchens with additional wall space. Corner units and tall pantries expand storage capacity, while narrower cabinets address specific needs, such as cookie sheets, plates and other thin or odd-shaped items.

Most cabinets installed in new production homes are called stock cabinets, purchased from local suppliers who represent one or more large cabinet manufacturers. The advantage of stock cabinetry, to both a builder and you, is three-fold: (1) Stock cabinet makers offer a wide enough variety of styles, dimensions and finishes to meet the majority of kitchen plans, needs and tastes. (2) Manufacturers keep the most popular cabinet styles and sizes in inventory, allowing for faster delivery. (3) And stock cabinets cost less than comparable custom-made cabinets.

Cabinets are ordered based on the dimensions and pre-determined layout of the kitchen or bathroom, as specified and drawn on the blueprints or working drawings for the house. While not checked by code officials, this detailing gives the local cabinet seller (and the manufacturer) precise instructions on the various sizes and finishes needed, thus directing the order to the factory or warehouse for production and delivery by a specified date.

**Cabinet installation
(kitchen and bath)**
Approx. time (days): 3
Cum. time (days):....64-81

Cabinet Installation

Delivered in boxes and labeled per the plans, cabinets are distinguished by a particular dimension and whether they are base ("B") or wall ("W") units. For instance, a box labeled "30W" indicates a 30-inch wall cabinet. The installer simply follows the plans and installs the cabinets in proper sequence along the floor or walls of the kitchen or bathroom.

If the walls are straight and true, and the floor is level, cabinet installation can be done quickly, perhaps within a day or so. There's no rule to whether the wall or base cabinets go in first, though some installers prefer to hang the wall units without being crowded by or having to work around the base cabinets. Before the boxes are installed, the fronts, adjustable shelves and hardware (hinges, and pulls) are removed and stored to protect them from damage and also to keep them out of harm's way during the job.

TAKE NOTE: Range hoods

Building codes often require ventilation of the kitchen range or cook top, which is typically achieved through a fan (with a light) over the appliance, also called a range hood. Often, the kitchen plan calls for a horizontal wall cabinet above the range hood primarily to conceal and protect the duct that attaches to the fan and carries exhausted air through the attic and roof to the outdoors.

Before the appliances are placed in the kitchen, the cabinet installer or HVAC contractor will cut a hole in the bottom and top of the chosen cabinet, often rough-looking gashes that appear to be careless in their execution. However, because the range hood underneath and the ceiling above will hide these holes, there's no need to make them look pretty. Once the cabinet is hung on the wall and, eventually, the range hood is attached, there will be little (if any) indication of what's going on behind the doors of the cabinet.

Wall cabinets are hung by long screws into the wall studs, requiring the installer to find the vertical structural members and draw lines indicating their location on the walls as he or she hangs each cabinet. Stock cabinets are usually lighter than custom cabinets (manufacturers use composite wood substrates instead of solid wood on most of their products), so even a few screws along a length of one stud is often sufficient to secure a narrow cabinet to the wall. If a cabinet misses a stud, the installer may use drywall anchors to attach the box. The best scenario, however, is to bridge two studs with a cabinet box.

The base cabinet install the same way, though without the hassle (or hazard) of having to hoist a wooden box five feet in the air and hold it while it is aligned properly and secured to the wall studs. Each wall and base cabinet also is secured to another next to it through adjoining frames.

Occasionally, the wall studs and floor might be a bit out of square, plumb or level, requiring the cabinet installer to shim (as the window installer did) the boxes to align them properly along the wall and to each other for a nearly seamless look. If possible, shims are located along the wall stud locations and are thus secured in place

A cooktop installed in the countertop turns this peninsula into an efficient cooking center.

Photo: Aristokraft, Inc.

TAKE NOTE: Kitchen islands

Wall and base cabinets are secured by screws into the vertical studs, but how are cabinets for a kitchen island anchored in place without walls to support them? Though perhaps specially ordered for an island (or peninsula) application, such cabinets are no different in their construction than standard base cabinets, with a bottom or underside frame that rests directly on the floor. Because plywood or OSB floor sheathing is structural, the cabinets can be screwed into the subfloor without having to hit a joist or other structural floor member. Shimmed for precise alignment, island and peninsula cabinets are also secured to each other through their back and side panels or frames, locking them together as if one, large cabinet.

Lingo:

island or peninsula—a work surface that is not set against a wall or extends from another into the space and is accessible on all sides (an island) or three sides (a peninsula).

as the cabinets are installed.

Sometimes (and mostly with remodeling jobs on older homes), shimming still can't eliminate a slight gap between two cabinet boxes. For those instances, manufacturers often supply thin strips of a material (or trim) that match the cabinet finish. The installer simply cuts it to length and width and glues it with a high-strength mastic to cover the gap. The edges of the trim strips, if even noticeable, should be concealed by the door and drawer fronts.

Shimming and extra trim work can add a day or more to a cabinet installation, and are affected directly by the quality of the materials and workmanship in the rough-framing stage (see Chapter 3). While there's not a lot you can do to correct a wall out of square or plumb once the drywall and finishes are applied, you probably will never notice the shimming and trim work necessary to make the cabinets look straight and true, especially once the cabinet fronts and hardware are put back on the boxes. And you shouldn't have any problems with their operation or performance.

Cabinet finish (kitchen and bath)
Approx. time (days): 1
Cum. time (days):....65-82

Replacing the hinges, hanging the door and drawer fronts and installing the pulls and knobs on the cabinets can be quite time consuming depending on the number of cabinets and whether the doors need to be adjusted to fit squarely and align to each other. Most hinges have a mechanism that allows the installer to adjust the door fronts up or down to achieve alignment, while cabinet

Photo: Wilsonart

Solid surface countertops offer a seamless, often more stable alternative to laminate or ceramic tile.

manufacturers pre-drill the holes for the hardware, mitigating the potential for splits while also saving the installer's time.

Countertops

Countertops
Approx. time (days):....1-3
Cum. time (days):....66-85

Aligned and flush to one another, the base cabinets provide the frame structure and surface for the installation of the countertops and other work surfaces in the kitchen and, occasionally, the bathrooms. In fact, most cabinet manufacturers accommodate countertops by installing triangle-shaped pieces of plastic in the corners of each base cabinet, complete with pre-drilled holes for the screws required to hold the countertop to the cabinets.

Laminate

In most new homes, especially tract or production houses, builders specify standard laminate tops, a pressed or composite wood substrate with a thin, continuous sheet of high-strength laminate veneer on the top and exposed edges. Cut and formed to the kitchen plan drawn on the blueprints, the counters arrive on site ready to install. Once positioned and checked for level, the tops are secured with screws from the cabinet frame to the underside of the counter. The trick, of course, is to use screws long enough to hold the counters tight to the cabinet, but short enough not to poke through the laminate surface. It is a simple calculation and the counter surface is rarely breached.

Of course, countertops are available in greater variety than just laminate, though that section of the industry has vastly improved its selection and quality since the freckled patterns of the 1950s.

Solid Surface

An increasingly popular material is called solid surface, in essence a countertop composed entirely of laminate instead of a veneer over a wood substrate. The advantage of solid surface is that its color or pattern is carried through the entire thickness of the top. Scratches and other damage often can be sanded out without exposing a wood substrate underneath.

Some solid-surface material is even more flexible, a cross between stone and laminate. Corian, a brand name of DuPont Corporation but now universally (and incorrectly) used generically for all solid-surface material, has the texture of a hard surface like granite or marble. In fact, it is a reinforced polymer material that is formed and moulded as a liquid, then cured to a tough, water-resistant, color-through material for countertops, sink basins and other household products.

Photo: Kohler Co.

Ceramic tiles are colorful accent pieces in a child's bathroom.

Because it is flexible when heated to a certain temperature, Corian and its derivatives can be made to look seamless in application. The installer simply heats up the joint between adjoining sections with a small torch or heat gun, softening and smoothing the material until the gap disappears and the sections merge chemically.

The ultimate solid surface, of course, is granite or marble. While Corian and other polymer-based surfaces do a fairly good job replicating the look of the real thing, stone still provides a unique texture and quality, albeit at a premium price. Solid stone also is heavy and awkward to install. For all those reasons, and because they can often achieve a similar look with a less-expensive laminate or solid-surface products, production builders rarely install granite or marble as a standard counter material.

Ceramic Tile
Lastly, ceramic tile is among the popular countertop choices, though it requires more work and time—a downside for most tract builders. Ceramic tile, however, gives a dimensional, classic look to kitchens and bathrooms.

Special tiles for edges, often in a bullnose or rounded shape, help finish off the job and soften sharp corners, while tiles along the back wall of the counter, extending perhaps a foot vertically, protect the drywall and other finishes from moisture damage (hence the term "backsplash").

Installing a ceramic-tile countertop is a three-step process, usually requiring at least two days to complete (as opposed to a laminate or solid-surface top that can be installed within hours). First, as with a tile floor, the material needs a solid backing or substrate, usually a section of ⅜-inch, smooth-surface plywood cut to shape and secured with screws to the base cabinets. Then, the tiles are laid out in their desired pattern, allowing the tile setter (a separate contractor, yet again) to anticipate what tiles will need to be cut and how to best conceal or minimize those instances.

Just like a floor application, the tiles are set in progressive sections so that the mortar doesn't dry out as the tiles are laid in their pattern. After letting the mortar dry overnight, the tile setter returns to gently scrub or scrape off any loose or surface mortar, then applies the grout, a slurry substance that dries between the tiles. Grout masks and strengthens the joints and conceals the mortar underneath. It dries within a day, completing the installation.

Time Frame

Whatever the countertop material, it is either installed before or after the appliances are set in place. The timing simply depends on the builder and the availability of the material and installers, as well as considerations such as under-counter appliances (such as dishwashers or microwave ovens), which are more easily installed before the tops go on. Still, some builders prefer to have the counters in before the appliances, if only to provide a final, finished height for the proper alignment of those products.

Mechanical and Electrical Finish

Electrical finish
Approx. time (days): 2
Cum. time (days):....68-87

Lingo:

backsplash—a protective, waterproof panel or apron against moisture, often behind a sink or countertop.

Before appliances go in, the builder typically calls the electrician and the HVAC contractor back to the house to finish off the rough work they put in place perhaps a month earlier. Scheduling these trades during the interior finish stage, though, is really a matter of choice and priority on the part of the builder or superintendent, or perhaps depending on the availability of the subcontractors. As with painting and flooring, the fewer finishes in the way, the faster an electrician and mechanical contractor can work.

Electrical

With strands of loose wires and bare outlets and switches sticking out from the wall and ceilings, the bulk of an electrician's job at the finish stage is simply covering up his initial work with ceiling and wall fixtures, light bulbs and faceplates. Even the installation of products with more complicated controls, such as dimmer switches and ceiling fans, are made easy because actual control mechanisms are already in place, tested and inspected during the rough stage.

That said, there are literally dozens of places in a house requiring electrical finish work. Every outlet and switch needs a faceplate; most every room has a ceiling fixture. Some areas have more complicated or complex schemes. The kitchen for instance, may call for a series of cylindrical recessed light fixtures (or "cans") for general lighting, task lighting under the wall cabinets to illuminate the counters and work surfaces, a hanging ceiling fixture over the breakfast nook table, and perhaps some additional accent lighting. An electrician's crew can be in a house for a day or more just focusing on those items. An electrician working alone may need a week to complete the job.

Often, the electrician and HVAC contractor are scheduled in tandem. Not only are they often able to work in the same house without getting in each other's way, the two trades may need to coordinate portions of their work. Ventilation fans in the bathrooms and kitchen, for instance, are electrically controlled, but require attachment to ducts. HVAC contractors, therefore, may tie a bath fan to its vent, but let the electrician strap on the wires to make it run. More commonly, the mechanical sub will be proficient and skilled enough to install the fan completely, with the electrician perhaps checking the work later.

Mechanical/HVAC finish
Approx. time (days): 2
Cum. time (days):....70-89

HVAC

Like the electrician , the HVAC contractor's work during the finish stage is mostly covering up his rough installations. Screwing in vent registers, installing mechanical fans and hooking up thermostats or other controls make up this portion of the job. The hard part was done a month ago. Still, because of the sum of these small parts, finishing the mechanical systems can take a few days.

On occasion, the builder may simply have a carpenter or work crew member do the work, calling the heating sub back only under special or complicated conditions or to test the finished systems and control mechanisms. But because most production builders rely on their subs, including the HVAC contractor, to supply and install the materials and products specific to their trades, calling the mechanical sub back to finish the job is often a matter of course.

Lingo:

dimmer switches—electrical controls that allow light fixtures to be dimmed rather than either on or off.

task lighting—light fixtures positioned and of sufficient wattage to illuminate work areas or countertops, subsidizing or enhancing the room's general lighting scheme in a particular area.

167

**Appliances/
plumbing finish**
Approx. time (days):....2-5
Cum. time (days):....72-94

Appliances and Plumbing Fixtures

Once the flooring and cabinets are installed, and perhaps after the electrical and mechanical systems are finished, the next step is to set the appliances in place and finish the plumbing installation.

Appliances

Like cabinets, appliances arrive on the job site in boxes and are often stored in the garage or other secure, covered area until the kitchen is ready for their installation. To mitigate the potential for damage to both the appliances and the finish work already completed inside, most builders will move them with a hand truck or dolly as close to their final position as possible before taking them out of their boxes.

To protect them from damage, kitchen appliances are often some of the last products installed.

Occasionally, the plumber will be required to hook up and test a gas line leading to a cooking appliance (gas range), the clothes dryer or the plumbing lines to a dishwasher, but for the most part appliances are simple to install, requiring no special skill or trade. Already, ade-

Photo: Kevin Berne

A finished kitchen encompasses just about all of the interior finishes required for a completed house.

quate electrical power is available, and products like electric oven-ranges and refrigerators simply plug in and start working. Most appliances are adjustable, allowing the installer (often a carpenter or in-house crew member) to set them squarely on the floor and flush with the countertops or finished height of the base cabinets.

Of course, the real trick with appliances is to install them without damaging the finished flooring, cabinets and countertops. Even if they are maneuvered into position (or close to it) still in their boxes, appliances are awkward to move once they are taken out for final installation. Sharp edges on their backs and undersides can rip a gash in a vinyl floor or the side of a cabinet box if not handled carefully. So, while it may appear simple to shove a range into place, there's often more to it than that.

Lingo:

in-house crew—workers on the builder's payroll, as opposed to subcontractors.

Plumbing

Finishing off the rough plumbing is one of the most time-consuming tasks of the interior finish phase, if only because there typically are so many spots in need of a sink basin, faucet or other fixture, each of which has to be tested for leaks, proper flow, adequate drainage and ventilation.

Though not a carpenter by trade or training, plumbers often install bathroom vanities (a solid section, often of cultured marble, that

TAKE NOTE: Home electronics

Of course, electrical, mechanical, and later, plumbing, aren't the only utilities that need to be finished in modern new homes. Sometime during this stage, often alongside or just before or after the electrician and HVAC trades, the various installers of the security, entertainment, telephone and data, cable and other electronic features must also return to the house to apply their finishes, from phone jacks to wall-mounted intercoms. As more buyers and builders insist on these gizmos, the time it takes to complete a new home lengthens.

Lingo:

vanity—a combination of a cabinet box and front(s) underneath a moulded, solid surface sink basin and countertop, typically in a bathroom.

cultured marble—an engineered and factory-produced composite made to replicate the look and feel of real marble, but which allows it to be formed into a variety of products, most commonly bathroom vanity tops.

Tub faucets (or fittings) are increasingly stylistic and convenient, with integral, pull-out, hand-held shower accessories in addition to the main spout.

Photo: Moen

includes a sink basin and countertop) and attach the kitchen sink to the countertop, requiring them to secure these products in place. Their primary job, of course, is to hook up the toilets, tub, faucets, shower fittings, clothes washer spouts and other plumbing products throughout the house. Plumbers often work in tight or awkward conditions and with professional care to mitigate damage to finishes such as chrome or polished brass.

Shower and tub enclosures It may appear simple and minor, but creating a separate shower enclosure (and, to a lesser extent, a tub-shower combination) often requires the coordination of several trades and may take up to a week to complete depending on their respective schedules.

The first component is the shower pan, a wedge-shaped slab of concrete or hard, thick reinforced plastic or fiber glass that slopes down to a drain in the floor (positioned there during the rough plumbing stage, see Chapter 4). In some cases, the tile setter or a carpenter will build a custom shower pan framed in lumber, sheathed in backer board (a reinforced, moisture-resistant sheathing) and sealed with a plastic sheeting or rubberized mastic.

Next, the plumber comes in to install the shower fittings, commonly a single handle or pair of knobs at waist level to control temperature and flow, and a shower head above, all of which ties in to the capped pipes placed during the rough stage. (Tub-

While most shower enclosures are built on site, some arrive pre-made for easier and faster assembly.
Photo: Kohler Co.

Pre-moulded shower pans allow a variety of shower enclosure designs and locations in the bathroom.

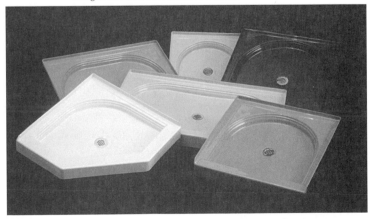

shower combinations, of course, also include a spout.)

Once the water flow and controls are tested, inspected and approved, the plumber moves out for the tile setter, who wraps the pan and walls with ceramic tiles in a pre-determined pattern and color, as well as adding accessories like integral soap dishes. Typically, tile setting on this basic scale takes a few days, as the tiles must dry overnight in mortar before being grouted.

During their installation, the tiles are carefully cut around protrusions, such as the handles and shower head. In fact, the tile setter

As in the kitchen, bathrooms require several finishes, from heating and ventilating to plumbing fixtures, flooring and cabinets.
Photo: Moen

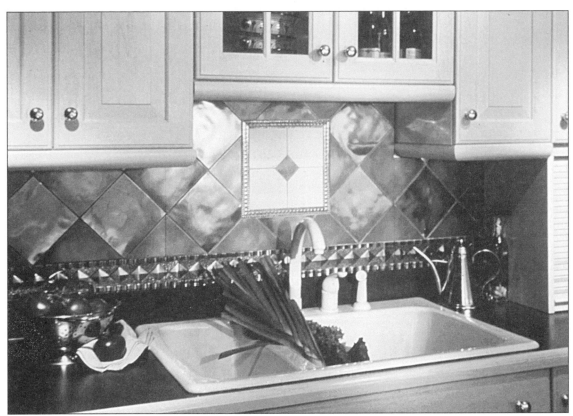

Photo: Moen

This isn't your grand-mother's tile: New finishes, including metallic and hand-painted tiles, add a distinctive look to kitchens and baths.

will likely remove the handles (if not the actual valves they control) to make more precise and concealed cuts. He or she then replaces the handles once the tile is grouted.

Finally, with the tile mortar and grout sufficiently cured, a carpenter or installer from the supplier hangs the panels and door that will enclose the shower, fastening the tracks or frame into the walls, pan and ceiling (if it extends that high), then positioning the glass panels and hinged door in place.

Occasionally, the frame for the shower enclosure is installed prior to the tile, thus ensuring a better connection to the walls and mitigating any chance of breaking a tile during installation of the enclosure. If the frame goes in first, the tile setter then works around it to finish the walls.

As you did in the kitchen, take quick mental stock of all the plumbing fixtures and fittings in your house and you'll get some sense of

This curving staircase is a microcosm of interior finishes, including trim, carpeting, lighting and paint.

Photo: Sherwin Williams

the scope of a plumber's job. In a typical house, with two and one-half baths, a modern kitchen, washer-dryer hookups and a utility or laundry sink—all of which must be tested, balanced and inspected by the building department, as well as coordinated with other finish trades—the plumbing finish can take perhaps a week to complete.

Accessory Items

Once the plumbing finishes are applied, though, the house is virtually done. What remains are the myriad accessories common in most homes, typically requiring the builder's carpenter or a finish-carpentry subcontractor to install. These items include towel bars and robe hooks, soap dishes, built-in shelving, bathroom mirrors and medicine cabinets, among other items and features. In addition,

Misc. accessories/ punch list
Approx. time (days): 2
Cum. time (days):....74-96

174

More and more, new homes feature myriad electronic systems, from intercoms to digital thermostats—each often requiring a separate contractor to install.

the builder or superintendent may have asked the door installer to wait until most of the interior finish work was done to hang the passage doors for bathrooms and bedrooms, saving those products from potential damage and repair, but also requiring another visit from the installer.

The installation of the carpeting, however, is often the signal that a new house is completed and ready for move-in. Of course, there are a few administrative steps still to go, primarily final inspections by the building department to allow occupancy, as well as a builder's internal inspection and a walk-through with you, the buyer, to catch any last-minute details or touch-ups (see Chapter 8). And, of course, you'll also have to close escrow with your mortgage lender and title company to take legal possession of the house.

Even so, if you stop by the home as the carpet installer loads up to leave for the last time, you'll find your new house looking complete and, finally, ready. ■

Settling In

Photo: Rich Binsacca

New neighborhoods often look new because the landscaping has yet to mature. In 10-15 years, however, the full value of the neighborhood will be realized.

Your new house is done. Whether the experience has been gratifying or a horror story, your home is finally completed. But is it okay to move in? Not yet. This part has probably been explained to you already by your builder, but here's a brief overview, anyway. There are a few administrative loose ends to tie up, including final inspections and formal walk-throughs, as well as punch-list items and other touch-ups before you can schedule the moving truck. Most are routine and for your protection, helping ensure legal transfer of the property and providing a final check of building-code compliance. This time also is one of the last opportunities to question your builder about the operation, maintenance and overall quality and appearance of the house before you take possession.

Other steps are more courtesy than conditional, and differ in their extent and approach from builder to builder. Savvy builders take extra time and effort to facilitate a smooth handoff to you, educat-

177

Photo: Rich Binsacca

Model home parks, distin-guished by an enclosed fence, feature the basic floor plans and products, as well as options and upgrades, offered by the builder.

ing you about service-call policies and procedures, warranty terms and general care of the house.

It is an important reminder that, for a builder, the transfer of title into your name marks the effective end of his or her job on that particular house. The best builders will, of course, complete the punch-list items in a timely fashion and respond to service calls and other questions that always emerge after move-in. But they gener-ally lack the emotional ties and excitement that buyers have for their new homes. Most are on to the next project or phase of homes in a development, often before your home is fully complete. There's no time or interest on their part to linger about, much less hold on to the baton.

Whether they build custom or production homes, builders often lack empathy for your relief and excitement (and perhaps a new set of worries) when your home is finished, just as some have a diffi-cult time showing compassion for your anxieties at start-up.

Again, for most of them, home building is a job. A single house is, in a sense, just another product shipped out the door. For that rea-son, don't expect your builder (especially a production builder) to be as excited as you are about the completion of your home. When you do and see something every day that most folks experience perhaps once or twice in a lifetime, it's a little difficult to get worked up over it every time.

Inspections

Every new house requires a final inspection by the local building department, called a "final" in builder lingo. While not a rubber stamp, the final inspection is typically routine, with the building official checking the validity of previous inspections on the card and generally ensuring that, once and for all, the building-code provisions have been met.

On final, the inspector will check all of the mechanical, plumbing and electrical systems (specifically the service boxes and any complex schemes), scrutinize the design of any staircases and handrails and examine the ventilation systems, among other items.

The final inspection also requires that the house be ready for occupancy. Therefore, the inspector will make sure that all floors are finished, light and plumbing fixtures installed and vent registers and faceplates attached. If there are any missing components, the inspector won't sign the card or approve the house for occupancy and must be called back when those items are in place.

TAKE NOTE: Improvement survey

Occasionally, you or the builder, perhaps per the title company, building department or the local tax assessor's office, will call for an improvement survey. Similar to the initial site survey that helped stake out the location and dimensions of the house before construction, the improvement survey maps the actual placement and dimensions of the building and other elements (property lines, rights of way, landscaping) now that the house is finished and the lot has been "improved." The improvement survey, conducted and documented by a surveyor, may be a part of the paperwork to gain a Certificate of Occupancy and/or to legally transfer title.

Though some aspects of the final inspection appear cosmetic, building codes are written and enforced to set the minimum standards for health and safety. They have nothing to do with quality or workmanship beyond any issue that might endanger an occupant. A "code-compliant" house may be well-built, but the two terms are not synonymous. For instance, an inspector won't comment on a gap between the wall and cabinets, or a poor trim job. That'll be your responsibility when you tour the house with your builder, called a walk-through (see below).

Once the inspector has signed off on the final inspection, the builder submits the completed inspection card (or set of cards, plus any other required documents) back to the building department for a Certificate of Occupancy (C.O.). Upon receipt of the C.O. by you, the homeowner, the process of transferring title and handing the house over can proceed.

Getting the actual C.O. depends on everything being done and whether there is a backlog at the building department. On occasion, anticipating a delay beyond your close of escrow (or settlement) date to issue the C.O., the building department may give out a temporary certificate contingent on the actual one proceeding through its processes and reviews, if only to avoid any hitches in getting you moved in or securing your mortgage loan or interest rate.

Walk-throughs

In addition to the final inspection and sign-off by the local building department, your builder also needs your approval.

The most common procedure to achieve this approval is the walk-through, a tour of the house after the final inspection to review the operation and maintenance of certain systems and products, go over any touch-up items, and generally give you an opportunity to ask questions about your new house.

Builders differ greatly on their approach to the walk-through. Many conduct an internal inspection a few days or a week before your final tour to fix any glitches, test the operation of various systems and anticipate any questions you may have. Those that pre-inspect often come to the walk-through with a punch list, a roster of items that will need to be addressed before you move in or soon after, as well as any other conditions to be aware of during your tour to head off any surprises or confusion.

Punch-list items include things like paint touch-ups, loose tiles, and missing or broken finishes such as a cracked faceplate or broken light bulb—mostly minor things that require an hour or two of a general carpenter's time. The list might be amended during your walk-through, and you should insist on a target date for getting items addressed to your satisfaction.

Photo: Rich Binsacca

The trend toward large luxury homes has led to a melding of architectural styles and rules.

That date might be before or after close of escrow or move-in, depending on when those events occur and your comfort level. However, it is important to realize that you have more leverage with a builder before close of escrow than after that date, when you are the legal owner of the home.

TAKE NOTE: Punch-list schedule

On occasion, builders will schedule a worker or subcontractor to address punch-list items based on an internal or pre-inspection before your walk-through, especially if systems are malfunctioning and can't be demonstrated properly during your tour. Overall, however, builders wait until you've had the chance to amend or add to the punch-list items before calling back the subs or carpenters to fix them. That way, those folks only make one trip to the house, not two, saving time and money. Bottom line: don't expect everything to be perfect during your walk-through.

There's no way to anticipate exactly how this entire scenario will play out in your particular situation, but ideally it goes something like this: The builder (or, more commonly, one of his sales representatives or superintendents) schedules a date for the walk-through soon after the final inspection and before close of escrow. Before you actually tour the house, you'll meet with the builder's rep to go over the purpose of the walk-through, your respective roles and responsibilities during the tour and to discuss any existing or known punch-list items.

At this time, the builder may also present a homeowner's handbook or manual, typically a binder or folder containing a variety of information and instructions about the products and systems in your home, warranty details and contact procedures and perhaps a list of the subcontractors or other local tradespeople who can provide emergency or routine service, if necessary. The handbook may also may include some courtesy items, such as a certificate from the painting contractor to return for touch-ups after you move in (as you're bound to scrape a few walls or baseboards) or coupons toward the purchase of furniture or other household items.

In addition, the builder might also explain his or her referral program, if one exists, including incentives to encourage you to recommend him to someone else looking for a home.

The actual walk-through can take from an hour to perhaps four hours, depending on the scope established by the builder, and is best conducted at midday when there are no shadows or glare to distort your view of the finished house, inside and out. Some builders formalize the process with a lengthy checklist; others simply point out known punch-list items and encourage you to jot down any notes or questions on a legal pad.

Either way, it is your responsibility to take charge of the walk-through, making sure you fully understand how to program the electronic thermostat, who to call when the furnace or water heater konks out and the correct wattage for the recessed lighting in the kitchen, among hundreds of other items.

During the walk-through, look for, document and identify incomplete or missing items, products or finishes that don't match the blueprints or specifications, malfunctioning systems or fixtures and damaged or unclean conditions. Also, point out flaws in workmanship such as gaps between finishes. Though involving a rather subjective evaluation, workmanship items often can be remedied and therefore should be added to the punch list.

General Maintenance Items

❑ Check smoke alarm operation monthly; replace batteries, as needed

❑ Clean gutters twice a year (early winter and late spring)

❑ Check the condition of the roof and siding (missing, loose or upturned shingles; nail pops, peeling paint and cracks) in the spring

❑ Make sure to "blow out" or otherwise drain sprinklers and outdoor water sources before the first frost (rule: off by Halloween, on by Easter)

❑ Change the furnace filter every 3 months and the air conditioner filter monthly; unclog the AC compressor cabinet louvers and hose away dirt from coils and aluminum fins; shade the unit, if possible.

❑ Empty and replenish spa or hot tub water every three months

❑ Re-caulk or otherwise seal openings as they wear over time (tip: use silicone-based sealants in wet areas, such as the kitchen and baths)

❑ Check the coils on the back of the refrigerator and freezer sections for ice and defrost with a blow dryer, if necessary; also, vacuum under and behind the refrigerator.

❑ Keep warranty and service company information handy.

The average walk-through takes about 90 minutes, after which the builder and you return to the sales office or sit in the kitchen and review the punch list again, often with additions or amendments from the tour. At some point, perhaps at this time or after the punch list is completed, the builder will ask you to sign off on the condition of the house and of its quality and workmanship.

TAKE NOTE: Setting Expectations

When you purchase a spec or production house, especially one that either is completed or already under construction in a subdivision, there's more risk that your expectations for workmanship and quality will not be met. If given the opportunity, work with your builder to set those expectations as soon as possible, so that there are no (or fewer) surprises or unmet expectations during the walk-through.

Again, the walk-through is your best and perhaps last chance to ask questions about your house before you move in. While many new homeowners are too intimidated by the building process or their builder to suggest or point out things they might think are wrong, regret and ill will after the fact are even worse feelings.

Warranties

By law, often at the state level, builders are held accountable for the condition and code compliance of their homes after the sale. This type of warranty is "implied," which means that it need not be written down or even signed by you or the builder to be enforced. Often, however, builders will formalize the process by presenting an "expressed" warranty, a written document outlining the terms and responsibilities for maintaining the house and addressing any structural or other needs within a stated amount of time.

Even the best builders, those you can call at home three years later to ask about a faulty faucet, need to eventually and expressly distance themselves from legal responsibility for the condition and performance of your home. If the house meets code and your expectations, there's no reason the builder should be on the hook for the house a decade later, except for major structural flaws or failure.

Though some are self-insured, most builders contract with an independent warranty company to insure the condition of the basic structure and main elements and systems of the house. Materials and workmanship are commonly covered for a year or two, while

Builders rarely furnish landscaping, though many new subdivisions require it soon after move-in.

Photo: Rich Binsacca

Photo: Rich Binsacca

Model homes are still the predominant way people learn about a new subdivision, but the Internet is a growing resource for home shoppers.

insurance for the performance of major structural elements, such as the roof frame and the foundation, may extend up to ten years.

Limited warranties of this nature are different from your homeowner's insurance policy and the separate warranty policies and paperwork you'll receive covering parts and labor on specific products, such as the appliances and HVAC system. Occasionally, subcontractors will offer limited warranties for their work, as well, though usually only at the request or requirement of the builder.

Warranties exist for your protection. Most go unused, either because the products and systems perform as promised or because homeowners resist asking for warranty service when it is needed or appropriate. Resist that reluctance by insisting that things work properly and consistently, and do your part to make sure you're not contributing to any flaws or failure from neglect or improper use and care.

Maintaining Your Home

At some point, either formally or unofficially, you have to start taking responsibility for the condition and performance of your new home. Builders shouldn't be expected to address every minor problem beyond the agreed service policies and procedures.

Part of your responsibility is knowing how things work in your house, and what to do if they fail or malfunction. With an increasing array of high-tech equipment in today's new homes, educating yourself on their operation can be daunting. However, if those products were demonstrated to your satisfaction on the walk-through or some other time, the builder is not your first phone call.

To help yourself, keep your homeowner's manual or handbook in a secure and easy-to-find place. If you have to create one yourself from the mass of paperwork you received, do so. It will contain all of the user manuals and service contracts for the various products and systems in your house, perhaps providing you with an easy and doable solution without the formal services of a technician or other tradesperson.

In a return to the past, some new subdivisions feature homes placed closer to the street, with the garages tucked in back, to facilitate a pedestrian-friendly neighborhood feel.

Photo: Rich Binsacca

Basic Tools

No one expects you to have a workshop in your garage or basement, but a basic set of tools is essential to help maintain your home and make minor repairs. And, as your interest and skill level increases, you can add more tools and equipment. Keep these tools and equipment clean and stored in a dry, temperate place, and replace damaged or broken handles and blades, as necessary. Finally, think safety first.

- ❑ 16-inch tool box (metal or hard plastic) with lift-out tray
- ❑ 12-16-ounce claw hammer
- ❑ 6-inch Phillips-head screwdriver
- ❑ 6-inch flat-head screwdriver
- ❑ 16-25-foot retractable metal tape measure
- ❑ 5 and 10-inch vise grips
- ❑ set of Allen wrenches
- ❑ clear-plastic safety goggles
- ❑ light-duty gloves
- ❑ 24-foot extension ladder
- ❑ step stool

In addition, follow the recommended maintenance schedule provided in many manuals or user guides to keep your house in top condition and working order. For instance, change the furnace filter every three months, keep debris off the roof, redirect the downspouts and splash blocks away from the foundation and keep the gutters clean, among other maintenance chores.

Equip yourself with a basic set of tools and equipment to fix things. Even if you're not handy with a hammer or a screwdriver, it helps to have those and other tools on hand to tighten a loose nut, reattach a foundation vent or open the service panel on the water heater to adjust the temperature.

A Final Word

It would be impossible to write a book that covers every base and possible scenario in the construction of a new house, and no attempt has been made to do so here. Rather, this book is intended to be a guide, to provide insight into the common sequence, methods and materials used in modern-day, residential frame construction, as well as the basic business practices and motivations of home builders and the construction industry.

Photo: Rich Binsacca

After move-in, warranty service includes follow-ups (or "call-backs") by subcontractors or the builder to either complete the job or make minor adjustments to certain products or systems.

All home builders want your experience to be positive, though some obviously fall short and a few fail to reach that goal. Hopefully, this book will give you the information you need to help bridge gaps in communication and expertise between you and your builder, easing any anxieties and smoothing rough spots during construction. The key, of course, is to realize that you have at least an equal responsibility to ensure you get the house you want, and to take action on that responsibility by working with your builder to achieve it. ■

Construction Glossary

2-by/4-by—the nominal size, in inches, of the narrow plane of standard wood framing components, as in a 2-by-4.

adobe—clay substance used to make unfired brick, which can then be stacked and mortared to create walls or other structural components.

allowances (code and budget)—in the building code, the acceptance of similar, if not exact, provisions that meet the code; in budget terms, an amount of money provided to the buyer for the purchase of certain items or products of their choice, such as appliances and light fixtures.

backsplash—a protective, waterproof panel or apron against moisture, often behind a sink or countertop.

bead—a continuous, half-round line of caulking material used to create a barrier between two materials or products, such as a window in a rough frame opening.

bird's mouth—the cut (or cuts) made at the end of a roof rafter or roof truss that allows it to rest on top of the intersecting wall.

bits—blades for a drill or drill motor.

bracing—a temporary support for aligning and supporting vertical concrete forms (for walls).

brick or stone veneer—thin pieces of natural or synthetic stone or brick material fastened to a wall or walkway to simulate full-size pieces.

casing—the trim work or moulding around a door or window.

chase—a space or area in the structural frame provided for ductwork and other utility conduits to hide them from view.

check—a split running parallel to the grain of the wood or lumber, caused by shrinkage.

cladding—a covering over a lesser-grade or vulnerable structure or material, such as a vinyl cladding over a wood-sash window.

close of escrow—settlement of the deed; when title and deed to the house and property are transferred from the seller (the builder) to the buyer or home owner after certain legal and financial conditions are met.

CMUs—industry abbreviation for concrete masonry units, or concrete blocks.

codes—standards of practice and design enforced by the local building depart ment to help ensure basic health and safety provisions and other protective measures.

combustion appliance—natural gas-operated appliances or equipment that rely on combustion air to fuel (or allow to burn) the natural gas.

concrete pour or "the pour"—the process of literally pouring wet concrete into the forms or other mould.

condensation—the formation of water from airborne moisture on a surface when temperature of that surface is below that of the air.

conduit—a hollow gateway, typically a length of pipe that carries and protects wires, water or other utility.

continuous load path—the integration of structural components so that loads are transferred from the frame to the foundation and soil.

control joints—in a concrete slab, strategically placed grooves to which cracks in the structure will gravitate, maintaining the structure's integrity and appearance. Also called a contraction joint.

countersunk—screwing or nailing the head of a fastener below the surface of the wood to conceal or protect it.

covenants—the rules of a community governing such things as landscape design, features and maintenance, house color and other items that impact the overall value of the neighborhood or community.

cripple studs—vertical members under the bottom plate (or horizontal piece) of a window opening; also used to hold up either end of a header across the top of a door or window opening.

crown—a natural curvature along the length of a section of wood. In concrete, a crown may be moulded on purpose to shed water away from the surface.

crown mouldings—an ornamental or decorative piece attached at the junction of the interior walls and ceiling.

cultured marble—an engineered and factory-produced composite made to replicate the look and feel of real marble, but which allows it to be formed into a variety of products, most commonly bathroom vanity tops.

cured—dry, as with concrete or mortar.

cut-off date—the last day a change can be made or a product ordered without incurring extra cost or delaying construction.

dimmer switches—electrical controls that allow light fixtures to be dimmed rather than either on or off.

door thresholds—a strip of moulded material placed on the floor between the jambs of a door to seal the door, facilitate a transition or change in floor finishes between rooms and/or provide weather protection.

drain tiles—a perforated, continuous perimeter pipe that collects and carries water and runoff away from the house to a drainage area (swale, ditch or sewer).

drywall—sheets or panels of pressed gypsum encased in paper; used to create interior wall surfaces.

duct—the conduit through which forced air (heated, cooled or exhausted), is delivered.

ductwork—the series of ducts leading to and from the furnace or other heating or cooling equipment throughout the house.

eaves—The bottom edges or other portions of the roof that extend beyond the outside walls of the house.

elevation renderings—realistic and to-scale line drawings of the home's exterior, as viewed from ground level.

engineered wood—structural and non-structural lumber that is made by reconstituting wood fibers, mixing them with resins and other adhesives and forming them into dimensional lumber as alternatives to milled or solid-sawn lumber.

equilibrium moisture content—the point at which the moisture content of wood or lumber is equal to the relative humidity (or moisture content) of its environment.

faceplate—a plastic or metal plate that fits over an electrical outlet or switch to protect and cover the wiring.

fascia—a length of wood or other material attached to the ends of the roof rafters or joists to enclose them, similar to the perimeter beam attached to the floor joists.

fixture—a product fixed to the structure, most commonly regarding plumbing products such as toilets, tubs and sinks, or lighting, such as in a ceiling.

flashing—protection against water or moisture infiltration, typically around roof protrusions and windows.

floor joists—framing components that create the structure of the floor.

flush—a surface that is flat or even with an adjoining surface.

footings—the part or section of the foundation that transfers and spreads the weight of the structure to the soil.

forms—the moulds into which concrete is poured to form walls, slabs and footings.

formwork—the moulds into which concrete is poured to form walls, slabs and footings.

framing cavity—the space, including the depth, between structural members, typically wall studs.

framing crew—the group of workers hired to build the home's structural frame.

freeze-thaw cycles—the systematic freezing and thawing of elements or products, such as plumbing pipes, which may result in damage or failure.

frost line—the depth at which the ground freezes in your area.

furring out—the use of non-structural wood or metal framing components attached to concrete or masonry walls for the fastening of drywall or other wall substrate or finish; in essence, a false wall or nailing surface.

gas line—the pipe that delivers natural gas or propane to an appliance.

GFI/ground fault interrupter—a device that ensures grounding of the wire to protect against electrical shock or short circuits.

glued veneer lumber—pieces of milled lumber glued together through heat and pressure to create a larger beam; also called a glulam beam.

grade—ground level, either natural or cut.

grade beams—structural members made of poured concrete that connect and reinforce structural piers.

grounding—the direct or indirect conduction of electricity to the ground or earth.

ground water—an underground source of water; an aquifer (as opposed to surface water, such as a reservoir).

hairline crack—a thin, slightly visible crack appearing on, but not penetrating the surface.

hip-style roof—a roof design where all sides are angled toward the ridge, creating a pyramid-like appearance.

honeycomb—a rough, pitted surface resulting from incomplete filling of concrete in the forms or inadequate tamping and vibrating.

humidity—the amount of moisture in the air.

hydrostatic pressure—pressure exerted by water on a structure, commonly the foundation.

in-house crew—workers on the builder's payroll, as opposed to subcontractors.

industrialized housing—factory-built or pre-manufactured housing that is either delivered to or assembled on a job site. Also, modular, manufactured or HUD-code housing.

installed costs—the price of a product plus the cost to install it.

island or peninsula—a work surface that is not set against a wall or extends from another into the space and is accessible on all sides (an island) or three sides (a peninsula).

lath—a thin strip of wood or series of strips attached to a wall.

lath-and-plaster—the process for creating interior walls before the invention and use of drywall in which thin strips of wood were attached to the wall studs and covered with a thin layer of plaster, which then dried to the finished surface. Gaps left between the lath helped secure the plaster to the wall.

lead times—the amount of time between ordering a product or material and when it is delivered.

light-gauge steel—steel components made from rolled steel as opposed to welded, heavy-gauge steel.

load—the weight of a given component or area of a house.

load-bearing—a piece or section that supports weight from above.

lumber load—the lumber delivery to the job site.

mason—a person trained to work with masonry, including brick and concrete block (CMUs).

massing—the overall proportion of a house and its features to the structure and the surrounding elements or lot.

mechanicals—a broad term referring to the plumbing, electrical, heating and cooling and other utility-driven operating systems in the house; specifically, may be used as synonym for the HVAC systems only.

mitered—a beveled or angled cut, usually at 45 degrees, at the end of a piece of wood or lumber.

model home—one or more homes built to showcase the floor plans and finishes offered by a builder in a speculative housing development, allowing prospective home buyers to tour finished and decorated homes before purchasing.

modular homes—homes in which the majority of construction occurs in a factory setting.

monolithic slab—a section of concrete created in a single pour or cast, with no joints other than control joints.

mortar—a mixture of concrete paste and aggregate (rock or minerals) used to connect or secure ceramic or stone tiles to a surface.

mortise-and-tenon joints—a connection between two pieces, typically wood, where a recessed cut in one piece (the mortise) receives a projecting cut from the other (the tenon), securing the pieces together.

nailing fin—a skirt or flap attached to a skylight, roof window, window or roof vent to help secure a product to the structure.

nail pops—the showing of nail heads in a finished wall, caused by shrinkage of the wood framing.

notches—sections cut out to accommodate another piece so that it is flush to the surface or relies on the first section for support.

on-center spacing—the distance between structural members, such as wall studs, floor joists and roof trusses.

open sheathing—roof sheathing applied or attached in long, thin strips (as opposed to full panels or sheets of plywood) with gaps between the strips to facilitate air flow from the attic to the roof finish.

optional upgrades—items, finishes or products available to a home buyer at extra cost.

pad—a developed piece of ground, or lot, upon which the house will be built.

panelized wall sections—sections of framed walls built in a factory and delivered to the job site.

pitch—the angle or slope of the roof.

planing—the process of creating or forming a flat surface.

planned development—a subdivision or newly constructed neighborhood of homes, starting with an undeveloped or unused section of land.

plate material—a horizontally set piece of wood used flat, or on its wider edge or face, at either the bottom or the top of vertical members, as in a framed wall section.

plenum—a closed chamber between the ductwork and the heating or cooling appliance that regulates the flow of air.

plumb—exact vertical, typically determined by a plumb bob (a cone-shaped metal weight on the end of a long string).

pre-built components—sections of a house frame or structure built in a factory and delivered to the job site, such as plated roof trusses and panelized wall sections.

pre-assembled form panels—formwork built elsewhere and delivered to the job site for erection.

primed—a product that is covered by a protective layer before finishing, such as with paint.

rafters—a series of sloping, parallel structural framing members that form the shape of the roof.

rails—on a panel door or cabinet front, the vertical sides of the panel frame.

rake—the overhang of a roof over a gable end.

rammed earth—building process by which a mixture of dirt, aggregate and water is hard-pressed into forms to create structural walls.

ready-mix—wet or "plastic" concrete manufactured for delivery; a mixture of cement, sand, and water.

rebar—reinforced steel bars set in wet concrete to add strength and stability.

return-air register—the vent and ductwork used to exhaust air from a room or area and either exhaust it from the house or return it to the HVAC system to be recycled.

rim joist—a piece of lumber that encloses the open ends of the floor joists.

roof pitches—the slope of the roof, from peak or ridge to the eaves.

roof trusses—pre-assembled sections that form the shape and structure of the roof.

rough-stake—a preliminary outline of the basic house to direct excavation of the lot or site.

scrap lumber—small sections of lumber cut from longer members during construction, often used in non-structural or support applications.

screed—the smoothing of a concrete surface, also called strikeoff.

setbacks—the distance from the property or lot lines to the actual structure (all sides), as determined by local zoning ordinances. Setbacks determine or regulate the space between neighboring homes.

set the forms—the process of building and reinforcing the formwork or forms in preparation for concrete.

settling—when sections of pavement or structures drop (or lower in elevation) because of their mass, weight imposed on them, or displacement of their support (typically soil).

Sheetrock—a brand name for drywall manufactured by United States Gypsum (USG) Corporation.

shrinkage—the contraction of a material due to moisture, cold or other climate condition.

single-family housing—a structure or dwelling unit built for one family, as opposed to an apartment building or duplex.

site superintendent—the builder's representative during actual construction, in charge of the job site. The superintendent (also called supervisor or foreman) is responsible for managing subcontractors, materials delivery and maintaining the schedule, budget and quality of the project.

sod—sections of grass or turf rolled out to create a lawn or other groundcover.

soffit—the underside of the rafters, often enclosed to protect the roof structure from moisture or other infiltration and hazards.

sound abatement—the reduction of sound waves through a structure.

spec homes or speculative housing—homes that are designed and built on the prospect of being sold during construction or upon completion, or on the "speculation" of an eventual buyer.

spotting a fixture—marking the location of or installing a product that is fixed to the structure.

spray-applied waterproofing—a polymer-enhanced membrane applied to a concrete surface through an air-driven hose and spray nozzle.

stem walls—foundation or other concrete or masonry walls resting on a continuous footing and extending only a few feet above grade.

stick-framing—industry term for platform framing, with "sticks" being the individual pieces of wood or steel used to assemble the structural frame.

stiles—on a panel door or cabinet front, the horizontal members of the panel frame.

straw-bale—building process by which bound bales of straw (dried hay) are stacked and reinforced to create structural, load-bearing walls and other components.

stripping forms—the process of removing the forms from the poured concrete after sufficient curing (or drying).

stubbed up—pipes or other utility conduits extending from the ground vertically and capped, which will eventually be connected to the home's various energy and water systems.

stucco—cement plaster applied to the exterior wall or surface of a building as a finish.

subfloor sheathing—panels of plywood used on top of the floor joists to tabilize and enclose the floor structure, creating a flat platform.

subs—subcontractors, also known as specialty or trade contractors, such as electricians, plumbers, framers and painters.

substrate—a backing for something else, such as paneling, ceramic tile or laminate.

subsurface drainage—the drainage of water, either natural or imposed, below the surface of the ground.

swale—a gently sloped trough behind or in close proximity to a house or houses that captures and carries drainage from rain, snow and other sources away from the property.

sweat pipes—soldering (or connecting with heated lead) metal pipe joints together.

tamping and vibrating—the manual and/or mechanical process of removing air pockets from poured concrete.

task lighting—light fixtures positioned and of sufficient wattage to illuminate work areas or countertops, subsidizing or enhancing the room's general lighting scheme in a particular area.

toe-nailing—inserting a nail or other fastener at an angle.

tract housing—mass-produced housing, typically in a subdivision or other planned housing development.

the trades—subcontractors or specialty contractors, such as electricians, plumbers and painters.

trim profile—the shape, design and details of the trim or moulding.

tripped circuit—the automatic disabling of an electrical circuit when it is overloaded or dysfunctional.

twist—a distortion of shape from wood shrinkage along two edges or planes.

V-ditch—a small, V-shaped concrete ditch used to collect and carry water runoff from one or two houses to a larger drainage area (a swale or sewer).

value-engineering—the process of evaluating the cost and structural value of a product or material to the overall structure.

vanity—a combination of a cabinet box and front(s) underneath a moulded, solid surface sink basin and countertop, typically in a bathroom.

vapor barrier—a membrane used to block airborne water (moisture vapor) from entering a space, such as a wall cavity or floor joists. Also called a vapor retarder or moisture barrier.

vaulted ceilings—angled or pitched ceilings, as opposed to flat.

walk-through—a buyer's tour and inspection of the house, typically occurring upon the completion of the home.

wall cavity—the space between two wall studs.

warp—a distortion of shape from wood shrinkage along one edge or plane.

washed gravel—small rocks that have been cleaned of dirt and other debris, typically used as a drainage medium under dirt and concrete.

water table—the topmost level of ground water or an underground aquifer.

weep holes—gaps left in masonry (brick, concrete block or stucco) to drain water and moisture trapped behind it.

wick up—the migration of moisture from one area to another.

wire mesh—lengths of heavy-gauge wire welded into a square-crossing mat and used to reinforce concrete slabs.

Index

Bibliography

Dwelling House Construction, Fifth Edition, by Albert G.H. Dietz; 1991, The M.I.T. Press, Cambridge, Mass.; ISBN: 0262041081

How to Build a Wood-Framed House, by L.O. Anderson; 1970, Dover Publications, Inc., New York; ISBN: 0486229548

Means Illustrated Construction Dictionary, compiled by Kornelis Smit; 1985, R.S. Means Company, Inc.; ISBN: 0911950826

Roofing & Siding, Lynne Gilberg, ed.; 1994, Sunset Books, Menlo Park, Calif.; ISBN: 037601492X

Rich Binsacca

Rich Binsacca is a nationally known, award-winning real estate journalist. His experience in home building began as a laborer for a general contracting firm while he attended the University of Missouri-Columbia, earning a degree in Journalism in 1987. He took that experience with him as an editor for *BUILDER* magazine in Washington, D.C., a national trade/business publication for home builders, where he focused on housing construction technology and products, as well as design and business issues.

After leaving *BUILDER* in 1991, he served as a project manager for a residential remodeling firm before joining the editorial staff at *The Practical Homeowner*, a national consumer lifestyle publication. He then moved to Boise, Idaho, to work for a small public relations firm, representing clients in the home building, architectural and building products industries, and also continued to contribute as a freelance writer to several real estate publications.

Since 1997, he has worked exclusively as a freelance journalist and author, co-writing *About Your House with Bob Yapp* for the syndicated PBS television series of the same name, as well as numerous other writing ventures. He currently resides in Boise with his two sons, Samuel and Nicholas.